THE VISIONARY POETICS
OF
ALLEN GINSBERG

BY
PAUL PORTUGÉS

ROSS-ERIKSON, PUBLISHERS
Santa Barbara
1978

Library of Congress Cataloging in Publication Data

Portugés, Paul Cornel, 1945-
  The visionary poetics of Allen Ginsberg.

  Bibliography: pp. 175-77
  Includes index.
  1. Ginsberg, Allen, 1926- —Aesthetics.
2. Ginsberg, Allen 1926- —Interviews. 3. Blake,
William, 1757-1827—Influence—Ginsberg. I. Title.
PS3513.174Z84   811'.5'4   78-6094
ISBN 0-915520-17-6
ISBN 0-915520-12-5 pbk.

Ross-Erikson, Publishers
629 State St.
Santa Barbara, CA 93101

ACKNOWLEDGMENTS

This book could not have been possible without the generous help of Allen Ginsberg. I would also like to thank Thomas Parkinson, Larzer Ziff, John Paterson, and Charles Muscatine for their encouragement along the way. Peter Whigham was a patient and thought-provoking editor, making sure that I dotted every "i" and crossed each "t." I am grateful to the Ford Foundation, the Fulbright Commission, and the Regents of U.C. for their aid while writing parts of the manuscript.

Dedicated to
Allen Ginsberg

Contents

Preface

...as I read William Blake
in Innocence
That day I heard Blake's voice
I say I heard Blake's voice...
*   an aural hallucination*
produced by the reconstruction of syllables on
*   the printed page in iron rhythm*
that rose to my ear in a
*   Voice...*[1]

—Ginsberg, 1961,
unpublished poem in
his journals

When Allen Ginsberg was twenty-two years old, he had a series of extraordinary visions that revolutionized his ideas about poetry, his concept of self, and his perception of the quotidian world. The primary purpose of Part I of this book is to explain, as factually as possible, exactly what happened to Ginsberg that eventful week in 1948 while he was under the spell of the poet William Blake's apparitional voice. The secondary purpose is to explore the far-reaching effects that these visions had on his poetry and his poetics. Part II is a series of conversations with Ginsberg in which we consider other important elements of his visionary quest: drugs, mantras, and meditation.

For a young poet living in mid-twentieth century America, the visionary path was a difficult journey to pursue. The mystic impulse in poetry demands a new sense of form, technique, and subject; it is also the cause of sudden and strange changes in personality and understanding, which in their turn induce a feeling of alienation. Nevertheless, for several years, Ginsberg answered the visionary calling and managed, after years of experimentation, to blaze a unique path for his poetry and poetics. Perhaps because of his "flamboyant" and mystical approach to poetry, Ginsberg has been ridiculed, neglected, and misunderstood by many apologists of contemporary writing. However, I hope this book will help create a more serious approach to his work, for I have tried as best I could to avoid the "ridiculous provincial school-boy ambitions and presuppositions... so lacking contact with practical fact,"[2] as Ginsberg has characterized a few previous interpretations of his poetry.

We are all prejudiced against the miraculous. The mystic tradition in Western culture has been avoided, suspected, or dismissed by a majority of critics. On the other hand, a small group has approached mysticism with a blatant, unquestioning acceptance—a sort of groupie, materialistic piety. The result of this kind of approach has been interpretations that are as difficult to untangle as the mysticism they have attempted to explain. In this book, I hope to avoid both extremes by simply presenting the evidence and by allowing the reader to assimilate the information as best as he or she can.

R. D. Laing has stated that any modern man or woman who experiences visions (and, like the tired Ancient Mariner, feels obligated to tell others about it) automatically is condemned as "psychotic." Ours is, after all, a culture steeped in scientific rationalism (note Blake's reaction to this fact: "Cast off Bacon, Locke, and Newton."). A few critics have even labeled Blake a schizophrenic psychotic, and, doubtless, the same "crazy" label has been applied to Ginsberg as well. Even

Blake's patron, Flaxman, probably flinched when Blake told him that he *knew* Milton, had seen him in visions, and that "Milton lov'd me in childhood & shew'd me his face."[3] Just as Blake's visions are a significant part of his poetry, so Ginsberg's visions hold a similar importance and should not be the subject of misunderstanding or ridicule.

The idea of a "vision" is a difficult concept to grasp without some attempt to narrow its application. "Vision" is, perhaps, one of the vaguest words in the language, tossed around by friends and foes of visionaries ever since Moses heard Jehovah's voice and saw God in a burning bush. Plotinus, one of Ginsberg's earliest models, makes the point that a visionary does not perceive a vision of an everyday reality. Instead, the visionary perceives by "another light . . . sees veritably," for

> the eye is not wholly dependent upon an outside
> and alien light; there is an earlier light within
> itself, a more brilliant, which it sees sometimes in
> a momentary flash . . . this is sight without the act,
> but it is the truest seeing.[4]

Oswald Spengler, another of Ginsberg's early mentors, makes use of Goethe's distinction that "the vision is to be carefully distinguished from seeing."[5] Blake also made a similar point when he quoted the visionary Isaiah as saying, "I saw no God, nor heard any, in a finite organical perception."[6] Blake himself, however, when he was a young boy walking about in Peckham Rye, "saw a tree filled with angels, bright angelic wings bespangling every bough like stars."[7] It can be deduced from these accounts, therefore, that a "vision" does not necessarily refer to ordinary perceptions of a real world (achieved by the use of the eye and its receptor and interpreter, the brain). In fact, "seeing" is not a *necessary* condition of a vision. Many of the great visions of St. Teresa and St. Ambrose, for example, were auditory visions, i.e., they heard voices but didn't see any supernatural spectres or even "bright angelic wings." Ginsberg's visions were primarily auditory—he *heard* Blake's voice. But, following his "auditory epiphany," he increased his powers of "true seeing" (in Plotinus' sense) several-fold, while experiencing a visual epiphany, a visual illumination of light that permeated the universe, and a heart epiphany of the ancient days, the father of man being present everywhere, in everybody always. So, in other words, I had a cosmic vibration breakthrough.[8]

Therefore, what is meant by a "vision" is confusing, because it is used by different people to mean different things. An objective definition is impossible precisely because the mystical awakening is such a personal, subjective experience with innumerable variables. However, in the context of this study, the concept of vision is taken from Ginsberg's own definition, as an "auditory hallucination" that can be accompanied by a "visual illumination," which results in the awakening of "extraordinary states of consciousness." In addition, an important aspect to remember is that a vision is a kind of medium through which the visionary experiences ontological perceptions that have a profound, lasting impact on the individual's life.

Most visionaries in Western culture have been Christians. However, one distinctive feature of Ginsberg's visions (and Blake's to some extent) is that they are directed toward the poetry and the poetics and *not* toward an ultimate, divine saviour. Blake would work himself into a visionary state and write poems based on the dictation of his "voices" and "true seeings." Ginsberg's visions were different from his master's in this respect. Instead of writing poems while under the influence of a visionary spell, he labored and experimented for years on a theory of poetry based on what he had experienced during his ordeal. In the late 1950's and early '60's, with the aid of psychedelic drugs, Ginsberg underwent similar visions without the guidance of Blake's spectre—all in the name of poetry and of his search for a "cosmic vibration." In fact, for more than a decade and a half, Ginsberg conjured up, rekindled, and finally renounced visionary consciousness. What, then, is the full meaning and explanation of his strange, transcendental illumination that became the foundation for such great works as "Howl" and the tragic lament "Kaddish"?

Part I

Allen Ginsberg's William Blake
and the Poetics of Vision, 1948–1963

Introduction

*The only poetic tradition is the voice out
of the burning bush. The rest is trash, and
will be consumed.*[1]

In the summer of 1948, Allen Ginsberg, at the age of 22,
had a number of visionary experiences under the influence and
guidance of William Blake's "illuminated voice." Like many of
the visionaries he had been studying—St. John of the Cross,
Plotinus, and Blake himself—Ginsberg heard voices, felt he
was in the presence of a Creator, and saw visions of a
preternatural light. The impact of these days and nights of
"awakening" was so compelling that Ginsberg spent the next
fifteen years, 1948–63, in quest of further miraculous break-
throughs in ordinary consciousness. He not only saw himself
in the tradition of visionary poets such as William Blake,
Christopher Smart, and Antonin Artaud, but he also believed
that Blake's "laying-on-of-hands" was a summons to a
meticulous investigation and exploration of unusual states of
awareness.

Ginsberg considers himself part of a tradition devoted to
the study of consciousness. In the twentieth century, Gertrude

3

Stein is the great model Ginsberg points to as the first modern writer dedicated to the systematic study of the modes of consciousness. He claims that Stein's interest in this field began while she was a student of William James at Harvard; James' main preoccupation in his work *The Varieties of Religious Experience* was the "pragmatic study of consciousness." Ginsberg believes that as Stein applied her Jamesian interests to her practice of composition, so he has adapted his visionary experiences to his theories of poetry and practice of writing. As with Stein's apprenticeship to James, Ginsberg's discipleship to Blake is part of a large-scale investigation (conducted by means of various experimental techniques) of unusual states of mind.

Ginsberg insists that the study of consciousness is the primary legitimate tradition in poetry:

> ...and I think that's a main legit tradition of poetics, the articulation of different modalities of consciousness... All that rises out of my preoccupation with higher states of consciousness on account of, as I said over and over, when I was young... some poems of Blake like "The Sunflower," "The Sick Rose," and "The Little Girl Lost" catalyzed in me an extraordinary state of mystical consciousness as well as auditory hallucinations of Blake's voice. I heard Blake's voice and also saw epiphanous illuminative visions on the rooftops of New York. While hearing Blake's voice.[2]

After the first of these visions, Ginsberg vowed to dedicate his life and poetics to the realization of Blake's demand that the poet must cleanse the doors of perception. He has even claimed that "almost everything I've done since these moments has [the Blake visions] as its motif."[3] In fact, he believes that the grave, earthen voice he heard that eventful night in his Harlem apartment is the voice—the actual speaking voice—he has developed and now uses when reading, singing, and chanting his poetry.

Ginsberg's poetics, then, must be approached from the angle of his Blake visions, since these visions dominated his theory and practice of poetry from 1948–63. The visions, in turn, should be understood as the point of departure for his studies of consciousness. Out of his visionary experiments, Ginsberg emerged with many of the primary theories and practices of his poetics. From his discipleship with Blake—a lady saint in India once told Ginsberg that he worshiped Blake as though Blake were his guru—he has developed a complicated and often misunderstood theory of composition, which he has labelled "First Thought, Best Thought"; a notion of his role as a poet; several ideas on the concept of prosody as a record of the movement of the meditative mind; a messianic identity, and a commitment to writing poetry as a record of the minute particulars of quotidian reality—as well as the minute particulars of the mind itself. In addition, the sense of a "cosmic-demonic consciousness" that Ginsberg was exposed to during his Blake visions became a major thematic quest in the poetry from 1948–63, particularly in the poems that are meditations on spiritual death and the dissolution of the body.

Part I of this study is a discussion of these subjects, beginning in Chapter I with a narrative account of each of the visionary episodes. Chapters II-V consider, in depth, the implications and significance of Ginsberg's visions as they affected his poetics and poetry. Chapter VI is a brief afterword in which are discussed parallels between Ginsberg's mystical experiences and those of some of the more well-known visionaries from whom he received much of his spiritual guidance—in particular St. John of the Cross.

I

Ginsberg's Visions of William Blake

That day I heard Blake's voice
I say I heard Blake's voice

—Ginsberg, 1961,
unpublished poem[1]

***

Now I'll record my secret vision,
    impossible sight of the fact of God:
It was no dream I lay broad waking on a
    fabulous couch in Harlem
having masturbated for no love, and read
    half naked an open book of Blake on my lap
Lo & behold! I was thoughtless and turned
    a page and gazed on the living sunflower
and heard a voice, it was Blake's reciting
    in earthen measure:
the voice rose out of the page to my secret
    ear that had never heard before—
I lifted my eyes to the window, red walls
    of buildings flashed outside, endless
    sad sky in Eternity,

7

the sunlight gazing on the world, apartments
of Harlem standing in the universe
—each brick and cornice stained with intelligence
like a vast living face—
the great brain unfolding and brooding in
wilderness!—Now speaking aloud with
Blake's voice
Love! thou patient presence & bone of the
body! Father! thy careful watching and
waiting over my soul!
My son! My son! the endless ages have
remembered me! My son! My son! Time
howled in anguish in my ear!
My son! My son! my Father wept and held
me in his dead arms.

—*Ginsberg, early 1960's*[2]

In July, 1948, Ginsberg was living by himself in a sublet Harlem apartment. He was in a very lonely, depressed state of mind. All of his friends were gone. Jack Kerouac, his tutor-in-prosody and spiritual confidant, was living incommunicado on Long Island, attempting to finish his first novel, *The Town and The City*. His intellectual mentor and amateur psychoanalyst, William Burroughs, was strung out on morphine in Mexico. Herbert Huncke, to whom Ginsberg was to dedicate his collection of early poems *Empty Mirror*, was in jail. Ginsberg had just received a very depressing letter from his lover and frequent muse, Neal Cassady:

July '48

Dear Allen:

You and I are now further apart than ever. Only with effort can I recall you. the last half-year has left an indelible print of an utterly different hue. (these are comma's—the tail doesn't show. poor ribbon) than that which you are a part of—in fact. to be presumptuous. I honestly doubt if you could feel my sadness ... What I'm trying to say: if you wish to share my intellectual life or know or deal with what I'm aware of. or concerned about—you're wasting your time and love. Since December I've cared for nothing. of late. as i returned. I came to see only one thing. whores. So. how can we talk of bitches? do you feel your belly

8

writhe when you pass a woman? can you see every
infinitesimal particle of their soul at a glance? at a sick.
loathing glance? —fuck it . . . Let us stop corresponding—
I'm not the N.C. you knew I'm not N.C. anymore. I more
closely resemble Baudelaire.[3]

Ginsberg has said that his visionary awakening was largely
a consequence of his depression resulting from the break-up
with Cassady. Cassady had been his "ultimate psycho-spiritual
sexo-cock jewel fulfillment."[4] The line from "Psalm IV"
(which stands as the epigraph to this section), "having
masturbated for no love," is an allusion to the then recent end
of their sexual love. By 1948, he and Cassady had, in Ginsberg's
words, "already been several years deep into a long physical
love affair."[5] Earlier that same year, they had been traveling
together, hitching cross-country to Denver. On the way back
East, they stopped at William Burroughs' farm outside
Huntsville, Texas. Burroughs was also Cassady's advisor and
friend. By this time, their money had run out, and since
everyone at Burroughs' place was broke, Ginsberg had to ship
out for Africa in order to earn some money to live on. He
arranged to meet Cassady that summer in New York. On the
money he made as a seaman, he hoped they could live together
and that there would be no shortage of funds forcing them
apart.

But Cassady never showed up. He sent the letter quoted
above. Instead of the promised reunion, Ginsberg was alone,
and he plunged into despair. He lamented the death of their
love in an early poem, "A Western Ballad" (1948):

> When I died, love, when I died
> my heart was broken in your care;
> I never suffered love so fair
> as I now suffer and abide
> when I died, love, when I died.
>
> When I died, love, when I died
> I wearied in an endless maze
> that men have walked for centuries,
> as endless as the gate was wide
> when I died, love, when I died.[6]

He was so dejected and hopeless living in his one room in

Harlem that he contemplated suicide. He even wrote the suicide note. In a letter to Kerouac he described his miserable state of mind:

> My soul does not want to take action, exist or die. I can't find the way out by thought, even action is useless it seems. My action is always balked and untrustworthy. I haven't even the guts or the clarity and resolution to pray for forgiveness because I am tongue tied and will not name my true sins.[7]

Not only was he faced with depression over the ashes of his scene with Cassady, but his mother, Naomi Ginsberg, had recently been incarcerated in Pilgrim State Hospital. Ginsberg has described his situation immediately prior to the first vision as not unlike the spiritual darkness St. John of the Cross deemed necessary as preparation for a visionary revelation:

> I'd given up on loves . . . given up in the same sense that St. John of the Cross says that when finally after seeking you give up, you go into a night of despair, a dark night of the soul.[8]

He had been reading St. John and felt he had certainly entered his own dark night of the soul, that he was not unlike the spiritual aspirant preparing himself for a visitation from God. With his emotional world fallen apart all around him, Ginsberg was alone one late afternoon in his apartment, in a state of hopelessness and frustration. His mind felt a strange, psychic equilibrium, "a funny balance of tension, in every direction."[9] Having just masturbated "for no love," his eye was idling over a page of Blake's "Ah! Sunflower":

> Ah Sun-flower! weary of time,
> Who countest the steps of the Sun:
> Seeking after that sweet golden clime
> Where the traveller's journey is done.
>
> Where the Youth pined away with desire,
> And the pale Virgin shrouded in snow:
> Arise from their graves and aspire
> Where my Sun-flower wishes to go.

He had read the poem many times before, but had thought of it as nothing more than "a sweet thing about flowers."[10] This time, however, while reading the first two lines, he suddenly heard a very deep "earthen grave voice in the room."[11] He became transfixed, somehow knowing immediately that it was the voice of William Blake speaking across the vault of time from beyond the grave: "I didn't think twice . . . it was Blake's voice."[12]

As Ginsberg experienced the auditory apparition, an overwhelming emotion arose in his soul in response to it. The emotion produced a sudden *visual* realization that helped him comprehend the meaning of this awesome phenomenon. He was, at the moment of the visual sensation, looking out through the window at the sky; suddenly, he felt, with Blake's voice guiding him, that he could penetrate the essence of the universe. He felt himself floating out of his body and thinking that heaven was on earth. He had a great realization that "This existence was it."[13] His sense of hopelessness vanished. He felt he had been chosen to experience a vast cosmic consciousness. Looking out of his window, the sky seemed very ancient. It was the "ancient place that he [Blake] was talking about, that sweet golden clime."[14]

Ginsberg felt a new sense of himself, a new role in life. Everything that had happened to him, the trials and tribulations of his affair with Cassady, and the loneliness he felt being cut off from his mother and friends, had been a necessary part of the spiritual preparation for his vision:

> —in other words, that this was the moment I was born for. This initiation. Or this vision or this consciousness, of being alive unto myself, alive myself to the Creator. As son of the Creator—who loved me, I realized, or who responded to my desire . . .[15]

The Creator had allowed him to see "into the depths of the universe."[16] His first thought was that it all made sense, that he was a chosen "spirit angel"[17] blessed by this vision of the universe. His second thought was to "never forget—never forget, never renig [*sic*], never deny"[18] the apparitional voice and the visual illumination. He swore never to get lost in the endless maze of superficial distraction, such as the mundane jobs and middle-class pursuits American life offers. Instead, he must, as a poet, always pursue the visionary calling, for "the spirit of the universe was what I was born to realize."[19]

Across the alley from his room there was an old apartment building, circa 1900. Ginsberg became transfixed by the craftsmanship of the cornices of the old tenement. They seemed like the "solidification of a great deal of intelligence and care and love also."[20] He noticed, in his heightened state of awareness, that in every corner

> ... where I looked evidences of a living hand, even in the bricks, in the arrangement of each brick. Some hands had placed them there—that some hand had placed the whole universe in front of me. That some hand had placed the sky. No, that's exaggerating—not that some hand had placed the sky but that the sky was the living blue hand itself. Or that God was in front of my eyes—*existence itself was God.*[21]

Ginsberg is here formulating his experience in hindsight. While he was actually looking at the cornices and bricks, the notion that "existence itself was God" was not a conscious or verbal articulation; it was a feeling that he had that everything he saw was a divine object.

The feeling of a divine presence, of a Creator or a God, was what gave Ginsberg a sense of cosmic awe about himself and everything he perceived. He began to have a sensation of light permeating his body. He suddenly felt suffused with *light* and experienced a sense of cosmic consciousness. While staring at the tenement cornices, he became aware of an immediate, deeper, real universe, an awareness which allowed him to penetrate the surface of things. He felt the doors of perception had been cleansed, that he was a living example of Blake's demand that the poet must widen the areas of consciousness and be able to see "Eternity in a grain of sand / Infinity in an hour."

Everything he looked at he saw anew. The bricks and cornices of the apartment building took on a supernatural glow. The sky and the light of the late afternoon became an "eternal light superimposed on everyday light."[22] Ginsberg characterized these perceptions as an example of Blake's dictum that the "eye altering alters all." He felt that the light had always been there, but until the vision he hadn't been able to see it. The vision of Blake's "Ah! Sunflower" had changed him forever.

***

Shortly after his first vision, Ginsberg heard Blake's voice again. This time Blake was chanting "The Sick Rose":

> O Rose, thou are sick!
> The invisible worm
> That flies in the night,
> In the howling storm,
>
> Has found out thy bed
> Of crimson joy,
> And his dark secret love
> Does thy life destroy.

Hearing the voice, Ginsberg became frightened. The awe and exuberance he had felt during his first vision was replaced by a dark sense of doom. Ginsberg thought that he was like the sick rose and that the prophetic poet Blake was seeking him out to make him face death. When he heard the last line of the poem, "Does thy life destroy," Ginsberg was convinced that the sick rose was himself and that

> Blake's character might be the one that's entered the body and is destroying it, or let us say death, some kind of mystical being of its own, trying to come in and devour the body, the rose.[23]

In this frame of mind, Ginsberg also felt that he was being instructed, not only about his own death, but about the "doom of the whole universe."[24] He became morbid, feeling as though he had no alternative but to accept the basic truth of Blake's message. However, once having accepted it, Ginsberg became aware that it possessed a strange yet inevitable beauty. He was scared and delighted, simultaneously.

Hearing the prophecy of doom, Ginsberg became convinced that he had been chosen to experience an ultimate

13

truth. The symbolic, obscure meaning of "this little magic formula statement in rhyme"[25] had been unveiled to him so that he could, as a poet, be party to the secrets that could deliver others, and himself, beyond the universe. Ginsberg had been given knowledge of death:

> ... my death and also the death of being itself, and that was the great pain. So, like a prophecy, not only in human terms but a prophecy as if Blake had penetrated the very secret core of the entire universe ...[26]

***

After absorbing the burden of doom he experienced from "The Sick Rose," Ginsberg had still another vision. He heard Blake chanting in a hypnotic tone the refrains of his poem "The Little Girl Lost":

> Do father, mother, *weep*
> Where can Lyca *sleep?*
>
> How can Lyca *sleep*
> If her mother *weep?*
>
> If her heart does *ache*
> Then let Lyca *wake;*
> If my mother *sleep,*
> Lyca shall not *weep.*

The effect of the heavy, masculine rhymes caused Ginsberg to go into a deep trance. His consciousness seemed to double, even triple in its ability to perceive hitherto untold knowledge about the secret meaning of things. He realized later that the repetitive sounds of the rhymes, with Blake's "earthen voice" chanting them, caused him completely to lose all sense of his body, normal time, and normal consciousness. It was as though he were under a magical spell, bewitched.

As he had identified himself with the dying rose, so Ginsberg thought that the little lost girl, Blake's Lyca, symbolized his deepest self, as well as his universal self. The mother and father seeking the lost child/self/Ginsberg were God the Father and Creator, and Blake. When he heard Blake chanting the lines "if her heart does *ache* / Then let Lyca *wake*," Ginsberg thought it meant that he was being called to

14

wake to a state of visionary awareness.

He knew his consciousness had expanded—miraculously—when he looked, once again, at the cornices of the apartment building. He realized he had an altered sense of perception:

> Which is what Blake was talking about. In other words a breakthrough from ordinary habitual consciousness into consciousness that was really seeing eternity in a flower . . . heaven in a grain of sand. As I was seeing heaven in the cornices of the building.[27]

He now saw the cornices as a communication of the eternal in a finite world. The intelligence of the workman who had laid the bricks communicated beyond time and the grave; there was a lasting intelligence, even beyond death.

With this new awareness, Ginsberg began to see everything as symbolic of an eternal intelligence. Before his vision, he hadn't even noticed the cornices, nor had he noticed the ordinary sunlight. The vision helped him see deeper into everyday reality. Ginsberg had never realized that everything—every object, every body, every *thing*—had sublime, spiritual significance. With his new consciousness, he now saw the cornices as

> . . . spiritual labor . . . that somebody had labored to make a curve in a piece of tin—to make a cornucopia out of a piece of industrial tin. Not only that man, the workman, the artisan, but the architect had thought of it, the builder had paid for it, the smelter had smelt it, the miner had dug it up out of the earth, the earth had gone through eons of preparing it. So the little molecules had slumbered for . . . for kalpas. So out of *all* these kalpas it all got together in a great succession of impulses, to be frozen finally in that one form of cornucopia cornices on the building front. And God knows how many people made the moon. Or what spirits labored . . . to set fire to the sun.[28]

This is the kind of awareness Ginsberg achieved on hearing Blake's voice, a sense of "total consciousness . . . of the complete universe."[29] It entailed the ability to see ordinary reality as a compendium of infinite, sublime meanings. It can

15

be compared to Blake staring into the sun and seeing, not only a bright, glowing, orange disc in the sky, but a band of angels singing holy! holy! holy! It's a perception of the sun (or of a cornice) that is, according to Ginsberg, "different from that of a man who just sees the sun, without any emotional relationship to it."[30]

***

For the next couple of weeks after these three visions, Ginsberg was in an exalted state of mind. Since it was 1948, however, he was faced with difficulties. There were no sympathetic acid freaks or post-1960 visionaries to whom he could relate his unusual experiences. At times he feared he might be insane. When he told a few of his favorite professors about the visions, they politely dismissed the story, thinking he was over-fatigued or had finally pushed himself too far. (Ginsberg already had something of a bad reputation around Columbia.) He was in a strange dilemma. On one hand, he might concede that he was somewhat crazed. But, on the other hand, what if his visions weren't imaginary freak-outs? What if they were absolutely "real"?

Despite his concern and uneasiness over his predicament, Ginsberg knew, without question, that he had changed. He not only saw everything with a new consciousness, but also his intellectual abilities had doubled. He was able to read obscure mystical texts, left in his apartment by a friend, and see "all sorts of divine significance in them."[31] He started re-reading the classics and concluded that great literature was an attempt at communicating extraordinary experiences, such as his own visions. Ginsberg was convinced that Tolstoy, Dostoyevsky, and many of the Greek and Egyptian writers, had had similar visionary experiences and that their great works were records of them. He thought that Wordsworth's theory of the sublime made complete sense and probably was based on a particular visionary episode, "not just any experience, but this [the visionary] experience."[32]

Encouraged by the visionary tradition that he sensed was the source of so much great literature, and still enchanted by

16

the "visionary gleam" he had himself experienced, Ginsberg began experimenting with conjuring up, like Goethe's Faust, the spirit of the universe—without the aid of Blake's voice:

> Then, in my room, I didn't know what to do. But I wanted to bring it up, so I began experimenting with it, without Blake. And I think it was one day in my kitchen ... I started moving around and sort of shaking my body and dancing up and down on the floor and saying "Dance! dance! dance! dance! spirit! spirit! dance!" ... And then it started coming over me, this big ... creepy, cryptozoid or monozoidal, so I got scared and quit.[33]

(In a manuscript at the Columbia Library, there is a notation by Ginsberg of this very chant. It was later incorporated into the poem "A Very Dove," itself an account of a Blake vision.)

Though Ginsberg didn't have much success in conjuring up visions without the help of Blake, he did have another visionary experience later that same week. He was walking around Columbia University one afternoon and decided to go into the campus bookstore. He started leafing through a volume of Blake and came across "The Human Abstract":

> Pity would be no more
> If we did not make somebody Poor;
> And Mercy no more could be
> If all were as happy as we.

> And mutual fear brings peace,
> Till the selfish loves increase:
> Then Cruelty knits a snare,
> And spreads his baits with care.

> He sits down with holy fears,
> And waters the ground with tears;
> Then Humility takes its root
> Underneath his foot.

> Soon spreads the dismal shade
> Of Mystery over his head;
> And the Caterpillar and Fly
> Feed on the Mystery.

> And it bears the fruit of Deceit,
> Ruddy and sweet to eat;

17

And the Raven his nest has made
In its thickest shade.

The Gods of the earth and sea
Sought thro' Nature to find his Tree;
But their search was all in vain:
There grows one in the Human Brain.

Suddenly, in the middle of the bookstore, the visionary feeling came over him once more, and he was in the eternal place again. He was experiencing the heightened awareness that he had had during his last vision, and he found himself looking, with a sense of awe, at the faces of the people around him. The bookstore clerk, whom Ginsberg had seen many times before ("a familiar fixture in the bookstore scene"[33]), now looked like a grotesque animal, a giraffe with a very long face. The man's face appeared distorted because Ginsberg saw beneath his façade and realized he was a soul in torment. He was amazed that he hadn't noticed the clerk's suffering before. He was also convinced that the man *knew*—knew how to see with a cleansed perception. It was apparent to Ginsberg that everyone he saw also had the same ability, but that they were all hiding it. Everyone had the potential for this kind of sublime perception, but each individual had fixed himself into a formulated posture and was stuck in his own self-deception, suppressing his visionary ability:

> They all had the consciousness, it was like a great *un*consciousness that was running between all of us that everybody *was* completely conscious, but that the fixed expressions that people have, the habitual expressions, the manners, the mode of talk, are all masks hiding this consciousness.[34]

He realized that the experience of his other visions was "too terrible" for most people even to acknowledge, much less pursue. He sensed that if everyone communicated on that awesome level of awareness, it would mean an immediate end to life as we know it. People wouldn't be able to carry on in the daily world any longer. The bookstore clerk wouldn't be able to sell books; money itself wouldn't pass over the counter; people

18

wouldn't even care about books, about having sex or whether anybody loved them, or whether their relatives died. The people he looked at seemed grotesque because they were hiding from knowledge of their death, from the sense of doom that had been revealed to Ginsberg. Therefore, they assumed postures and conducted their lives as if in a masquerade, following habitual conduct with forms to fulfill and roles to play.

But the main insight Ginsberg had at the time was "that everybody knew. Everybody knew completely everything. Knew completely everything in terms which I was talking about."[35] Yet, no one had the courage to face the forbidden knowledge. The torment on their faces was an expression of their repressed consciousness combined with a fear of rejection if they told anyone about their secret insight. People hated themselves because they couldn't face what they knew. This caused a common "disbelief in the infinite self,"[36] the same self that Ginsberg had been made conscious of in his vision of Blake's "The Little Girl Lost." Blake's lines from "London," "On every face I see, I meet / marks of weakness, marks of woe," ran through Ginsberg's mind. He concluded that everyone was hiding out of fear—a fear, in his words, of "total feeling, really, total being, is what it is."[37] Even as a poet, it was a difficult awareness to communicate. He immediately started wondering if, and how, he could safely manifest and communicate this new awareness without everyone's rejecting his secret vision. It was as though Blake's poem, "The Human Abstract," had come to life, with "Cruelty" giving rise to "Mystery" and bearing "the fruits of Deceit."

***

The next and last time Ginsberg had a vision was a week later. Again, he was walking around Columbia University in the field near the main library. He started invoking Blake's spirit, somewhat in the fashion he had the previous week in his kitchen. He managed to achieve a sense of "cosmic awareness" similar to his vision of "The Sick Rose," but the consciousness with which he was visited was altogether overwhelming. It was as if a hand of death were descending from the sky instead

19

of the beautiful blue hand of God he had seen before. Then a "really scary presence"[38] appeared, as if God or Blake had been supplanted by the Devil himself: "The consciousness itself was *so* vast . . . that it didn't even seem human any more."[39] He felt that perhaps he had gone too far. Though Ginsberg's commitment to Blake demanded that he blaze a "Western path / Right thru the Gates of Wrath,"[40] for the time being, he couldn't urge himself to pursue his visionary consciousness any further. He needed time to assimilate the visions, their impact, their meaning, their significance. Years later, in a boastful mood, he would confess that the visions were "glimpses of what I feel now, all the time":[41]

> And the voice I heard, the voice of Blake, the ancient saturnal voice, is the voice I have now. In other words, I was imagining my own potential awareness from a limited more virginal shy tender blossom of feeling. I was imagining the total power and feeling and universe possible to me.[42]

II

Ginsberg's Vision of Blake's "Ah! Sunflower"

and I heard a physical voice
not hallucination
except hallucinations be real—
that voice O Sunflower weary
of time...

—Ginsberg, unpublished poem,
April 13, 1961[1]

***

"Holy are the visions of the soul..."

—Ginsberg, from "Psalm," *The Gates of Wrath*[2]

The weeks and months following Ginsberg's days and nights of vision were a complete turmoil to him. He has characterized himself at that time as not unlike Coleridge's Ancient Mariner, compelled to stop whomever he could and tell them about his strange, horrific vision. Unfortunately, almost everyone Ginsberg told thought he was either on the verge of an emotional breakdown or that he must be making it all up. One of his professors at Columbia, the poet Mark Van Doren, was more sympathetic. Van Doren advised him to give up his visionary quest, for fear of going beyond the limits of what his reason could bear. Even Kerouac thought that Ginsberg had become some kind of messianic fanatic conjuring visions of angels, but he was too busy with his own work to take him very seriously. (A time would come, however, when Kerouac, in response to his monk-like practices in the Buddhist Hinayana and Mahayana schools, would undergo a series of visions himself, and his attitude to Ginsberg's experiences would change.) Later, in 1958, Ginsberg wrote a poem that, half-humorously, records his neurotic attempt of a decade earlier to tell people about his magnificent visions. It is titled "The Lion for Real," with Blake appearing as a symbolic lion chasing the young Ginsberg around trying to consume him:

> I came home and found a lion in my living room
> Rushed out on the fire-escape screaming Lion! Lion!
> Two stenographers pulled their brunette hair
>   and banged the window shut . . .
>
> Called up my old Reichian analyst
> who'd kicked me out of therapy for smoking
>   marijuana
> 'It's happened' I panted 'There's a lion in my
>   room'
> 'I'm afraid any discussion would have no value'
>   he hung up.[3]

The incidents and the people described in these two stanzas are based on actual situations. The poem reflects the desperate situation Ginsberg found himself in when he told people about his visions and nobody would believe him. Even his psychoanalyst wasn't very sympathetic. Several months later, as a result of his reputation as a "crazy," and because he had been arrested for possession of illegal drugs, Ginsberg was admitted to Rockland State Hospital for an eight month stay. It was the only way he could avoid prison; however, by that time, he was also questioning his own sanity since no one would accept what had happened to him those eventful days and nights in Harlem and at Columbia.

Despite his emotional imbalance, Ginsberg remained committed to his vow never to forget the truths of his Blake visions:

> But I also said at the time, now that I have seen this heaven on earth, I will never forget it, and I will never stop referring all things to it, I will never stop considering it the center of my human existence and the center of my life which is now changed—over the boundary and into the new world, and I'll never be able to go back and that's great, and from now on I'm chosen, blessed, sacred, poet, and this is my sunflower, or this is my new world, and I'll be faithful for the rest of my life, and I'll never forget it and I'll never deny it, and I'll never renounce it.[4]

Being faithful to the "sunflower," in terms of his poetry, meant that he was determined to work out a poetics of vision, a theory and practice of poetry that would allow him to communicate his visions and his heightened awareness of reality to an audience bent on denying the mundane as well as the sublime.

At first, Ginsberg thought the answer lay in successfully recreating the cosmic consciousness of his vision in his poems. All he had to do was write about the vision itself, and the reader would grasp the nuances and essence of the experience. But how could he accomplish that task? He turned to Blake for practical guidance. He understood very well Blake's own difficulties with his contemporaries, who also thought he was crazy and who were suspicious of his insistence that he wrote his poetry while under the power of a visionary trance. Ginsberg was encouraged when he read that Blake ignored his critics and devoted his energies to the problem of transposing visions into great poetry. Blake knew it would demand a complicated and highly sophisticated method, things "unattempted yet in Prose or rhyme," as Milton, Blake's own model of the poet as visionary, once stated in *his* experiments with the poetry of vision. For years, Blake pondered the problem of writing poetry based on vision. When he wrote his friend Thomas Butts on April 25, 1803, that he had written a long visionary poem, *Milton*, "from immediate Dictation . . . without Premeditation & even against my Will,"[5] he anticipated a tradition of automatic writing, later picked up by Yeats, the Surrealists, and the Beats. Whether he had in fact worked out the problem of creating a poetics based on vision is another question, but it seemed to Ginsberg that he had. Ginsberg was particularly impressed by Blake's final statement on his experiments in poetry "conducted by the Spirits," which he had read in the preface to *Jerusalem*. By this time, in his development as a poet, Blake was completely confident that he had discovered a poetics of vision, and his manifesto on prosody is a strong affirmation of his quest to write a poetry "unfettered" by habitual tradition and contemporary critical standards:

> We who dwell on Earth can do nothing to ourselves; everything is conducted by Spirits, no less than Digestion or Sleep. *I fear the best . . . in Jesus whom we . . .* When this Verse was first dictated to me, I consider'd a Monotonous Cadence, like that used by Milton & Shakespeare & all writers of English Blank Verse, derived from the modern bondage of Rhyming to be a necessary and indispensible part of Verse. But I soon found that in the mouth of the true Orator such monotony was not only awkward, but as much a bondage as rhyme itself. I therefore have produced a variety of syllables. Every word and every letter is studied and put into its fit place; the terrific numbers are reserved for the terrific parts, and the prosaic for inferior parts; all are necessary to each other. Poetry Fedder'd Fetters the Human Race.[6]

Like Blake, Ginsberg's difficult and long search for a new poetics would eventually produce his own great innovative work, "Howl," which he claims was possible because of his vow to Blake that he would write without fear of the consequences:

> I depended on the word "who" to keep the beat, a base to keep measure, turn to and take off from again on another streak of invention . . . continuing to prophesy what I really knew despite the drear consciousness of the

world . . . I went on to what my imagination believed true to Eternity (for I'd had a beautific illumination years before during which I'd heard Blake's ancient voice and saw the universe unfold in my brain . . .).[7]

"Howl" itself is a visionary record of Ginsberg's illumination of the hellish American underground in the late forties and early fifties. But, like Blake, Ginsberg had to struggle through years of experimentation to produce his great poem of the mid-fifties; and, it would take years of dedication and scores of lesser poems—poems mostly still unread even by Ginsberg's followers—to arrive at a poem that was "true to Eternity."

Ginsberg's first experiments in developing his poetics of vision began with several poems that attempt to record, retell, and recapture his visionary experiences under the guidance of Blake's spectral voice. After a year of writing poems exclusively about his visions, Ginsberg explored other aspects of his mystical illumination: his preoccupation with being in the presence of the Creator and yearning to get back that feeling of the infinite. After another year of devoting himself to poems with this dominant theme, Ginsberg began a masochistic phase in which he realized he couldn't attain "Heaven on Earth"; consequently, during 1950 and 1951 (two to three years after the original visions), Ginsberg devoted his poetry to the theme of renouncing life and merging with the infinite. This last phase was a classic poetic situation that most visionaries experience, i.e., giving up on life and wishing to die in order to be near, or in the presence of, the Creator.

By 1951, Ginsberg realized that he had not been very successful in developing his poetics of vision, that he had spent three years of spiritual exploration seeking a true Eternity— only to discover a frightening desire for his own death. He spent several months re-evaluating his visions, and, with the aid of Kerouac, William Carlos Williams, and others, he restructured his poetics. These three years of misdirection, interesting in themselves, provide an instructive prelude to any reconstruction of the fascinating period of self-discovery that led Ginsberg out of his spiritual and literary chaos and pointed him

25

in the direction of his great poetry of the mid- and late-fifties.

***

The first poem that Ginsberg wrote after his weeks of illumination exemplified the pattern of the poetry that he would design for at least the entire next year—well into 1949. It was one of a dozen poems that were a direct reference to his visionary experience. "The Eye Altering Alters All" is a dense, highly symbolic attempt to assert that everyone could have visions if they would conquer their prejudice against the miraculous and cease to deny the visionary seed in all of us:

> Many seek and never see,
> Anyone can tell them why.
> O they weep and O they cry
> and never take until they try
> unless they try it in their sleep[8]

The "it" in the last line that "many seek" but never try is the visionary consciousness. Ginsberg was convinced that people would be open to visions if he introduced the idea into the general stream of thought and encouraged others to try it:

> I thought that perhaps there was some element, you could catalyze it if you were willful or if you really threw yourself into the search for vision, you could bring it about. "Unless they try it in their sleep..." How many people had visionary experiences in dream? Has anybody *not* had a visionary experience in a dream?[9]

Though his own vision was definitely not a dream, Ginsberg thought people would accept the possibility of vision if they realized that a similar quality of experience existed in dreams.

Ginsberg's first attempt to recreate his visionary feeling came in a sonnet, "I dwelled in Hell on earth to write this rhyme." Like many of the poems of this period, most of which were not published until 1972 in *The Gates of Wrath*, the style is Elizabethan and metaphysical, reflecting the influence of his early models, Wyatt, Marvell, and Surrey. The poem is decorative, overwritten, full of conceits and poetic diction, with frequent reference to angels, infernos, and even a "blazing

26

stair"—all in the style of the sixteenth and seventeenth century mystics and sonneteers:

> The fame I Dwell in is not mine,
> I would not have it. Angels in the air
> Serenade my senses in delight.
> Intelligence of poets, saints and fair
> Characters converse with me all night.[10]

It is as though he were trying to capture the "visionary gleam" by copying the forms and styles of his mystic predecessors, such as the Vaughans, St. John of the Cross, and others. Ginsberg would later characterize this phase of his writing as "overwritten coy stanzas, a little after Marvell, a little after Wyatt."[11] He was consciously trying to perfect a rhymed, punning, "silvery" versification. This was an important effort in prosody that paralleled his misdirection in the search for supernatural realities; he would realize later that he would have to abandon both preoccupations in order to get back to the true spirit of Blake and his spiritual revelations.

For the next three years, however, Ginsberg wouldn't heed Blake's warning that a poet should abandon rhyme and syncopated meter when it meant bondage to the form rather than allegiance to truth. Therefore, his poems, like the above lines quoted from the sonnet, would be obscure, extremely allusive, and often archaic. A reader would have a hard time understanding what was meant by the "Intelligence of poets," or "Angels in the air," and particularly the vision of mystical light alluded to in the final line, "They vanish as I look into the light." Even with the hindsight of his Harlem experiences, it is difficult to know that "I witness Heaven" alludes to his vision of "Ah! Sunflower" and the heightened perception of the cornices and the late afternoon sunlight that seemed eternal, heavenly.

But Ginsberg was as committed as Blake to becoming a spiritual revolutionary, whose task it is "to explore and record the mysteries of the Human psyche."[12] So, he continued, as best he knew how, retelling his vision, as in the poem "Vision 1948," convinced that, since his annointment by the light, he

27

was "a poet with something to talk about":[13]

> I shudder with intelligence and I
> Wake in the deep light
> And hear a vast machinery
> Descending without sound,
> Intolerable to me, too bright,
> And shaken in the sight
> The eye goes blind before the world goes round.
> —*East Harlem, summer 1948*[14]

In this poem, Ginsberg is trying to communicate to the reader a sense of his Blake vision, as well as attempting to portray a feeling for the cosmic that he assumes, or hopes, might be understood by others. He later characterized this poem as a hermetic communication which he hoped could be appreciated at a deeper, perhaps unconscious, level of thought. In fact, he thought all his poetry should move toward the miraculous, the truly universal experiences of a higher state of being:

> I immediately saw poetry as a hermetic or secret way of talking about experiences that were universal, cosmic, that everybody knew about, but nobody knew how to refer to, nobody knew how to bring it up to front brain consciousness or to present it to social consciousness . . .[15]

Though he assumed "everybody knew about" the cosmic, he wasn't aware that the opaque allusions to his own experience of the mystical light—"Wake in the deep light"—or his sense of cosmic intelligence—"shudder with intelligence"—were clouded by his transmission of the eternal truths in a style difficult for the average reader to comprehend.

Ginsberg would continue to write poems in this fashion for the next year and a half. At least nine poems about his Blake vision were written in 1948 and 1949. The list includes, other than those already discussed, "A Very Dove," "Do We Understand Each Other?," "The Voice of Rock," "A Western Ballad," "On Reading William Blake's 'The Sick Rose',"—and a few others in his journals and letters.[16] However, after all these attempts, Ginsberg began to have second thoughts about

28

writing almost all his poems solely on the subject of his vision. He was gradually becoming aware of the sad fact that no one was taking him seriously, that many were even beginning to express doubts about his sanity. The strangeness of his experience, no less than the turgidity of his style, prevented him in these poems from opening people up to that sense of a cosmic consciousness that was his urgent aim. Consequently, he decided to approach the subject of his visions from another angle, emphasizing those aspects that people might be able to apply to themselves. He found that the general quality of vision itself was completely misunderstood. Even what he had thought was a well-known and well-documented experience—the sensation of light felt by all mystics—was met with bewilderment and doubt by his few readers (either his friends or his teachers). He decided to write a poem about this lack of ability to communicate. It is called "Refrain":

> The air is dark, the night is sad,
> I lie sleepless and I groan.
> Nobody cares when a man goes mad:
> He is sorry, God is glad.
> Shadow changes into bone.[17]

Ginsberg is confessing that nobody cares that he is a visionary and has been given access to unusual insights and eternal truths. His quest had only produced sleepless nights and groaning. The last line "Shadow changes into bone" is impossible to understand without Ginsberg's own gloss:

> "Shadow changes into bone" was my symbolic language
> for meaning Thought, high intellectual thought, ambition,
> idealized desire, and that it can actually come true and you
> do get to see a vision of eternity which kills you. So
> shadow, mind, insight changes into three dimensional
> bone.[18]

In other words, his "high intellectual thought"—the "vision of eternity"—changes from the ecstatic, epiphanous experience into a state of madness, eventually driving the mad visionary to the grave because of his inability to communicate his secret truths. By this time, the great intelligence, the amazing light, had been reduced to a shadow, the burden of which was killing him—"Shadow changes into bone."

Ginsberg's change of direction, therefore, resulted in an abandonment of visionary wonders for a desire to be in the presence of the Creator or Divinity, a state he thought most serious, spiritually-minded people would recognize:

> So by this time, a year later, the actual experience had become solidified into the symbol of a god, or the notion of a divinity that I was trying to get to.[19]

The poem that reflects this new focus is "Psalm." Ginsberg did not stop referring to his vision. (He would allude to it throughout the 1950's and 1960's in such poems as "Howl" and "Kaddish.") There are several passages that refer to his desire to infuse the "speechless stanzas of the rose / Into my poem." He is still making a vow to "copy / Every petal on a page" (alluding to his vision of "The Sick Rose") and claiming "Holy are the Visions of the Soul." But the interest of "Psalm" is the question—put rather straightforwardly toward the end of the penultimate stanza—"Am I to spend / My life in praise of the idea of God?" The conclusion is a resounding "yes," with Ginsberg making a new claim to praise the sense of divinity he had felt in his vision by making "the myth incarnate in my flesh," which in the last line of the poem is "Now made incarnate in Thy Psalm, O Lord."[20]

"Psalm" is an interesting poem in two respects. First, Ginsberg modeled it on the classical Christian visionary who, in order to re-experience the presence of the Creator, renounced "this life" in an attempt to achieve more rapidly a promised union with the light/God. Ginsberg had read of this desire and praise of divinity in James' *The Varieties of Religious Experience,* in St. John of the Cross, in St. Teresa, and even in some of the English mystic poets, such as Crashaw and Henry Vaughn. He was now experiencing the mystical death-wish himself. It was part of his desire to draw closer to that sense of cosmic awe one felt in the presence of one's Creator. It was partly also a response to the situation of complete alienation he was experiencing. Into the summer of 1951 Ginsberg would write about his "masochistic" wish, as he did in the following poem written in late 1949, "Complaint of the Skeleton To Time":

> Take the art which I bemoan
> In a poem's crazy tone;
> Grind me down, though I may groan,
> To the starkest stick and stone;
> Take them, said the skeleton
> But leave my bones alone.[21]

He was calling upon death in order to complete the inevitable cycle of his spiritual annointment by renouncing his loves, his thoughts, his earthly possessions in each successive stanza until the last (quoted above), where he even casts aside his poetry: "Take the art which I bemoan / In a poem's crazy tone."

Ginsberg has described this predicament in which he was trapped by his desire to enter the cosmic and eternal, regardless of the consequences:

> So then, after a while, the big masochistic psalms of divinity saying I want to die and be part of You. Which is a classic poetic position, which a lot of people get into, trapped into and finally die, too. Thinking, well, I'm going to pursue the beauty to the tomb. So: "Complaint of the Skeleton to Time."[22]

He would bemoan this aspect of his vision in poems such as "Sometime Jailhouse Blues" and "An Imaginary Rose in a Book," with such images as "tears of death," "body to a tomb," and "myth of dust," which illustrate the difficult and obscure style of the earlier poems.

It wasn't until the summer of 1951 that Ginsberg began to realize that he must put an end to this aspect of the visionary cycle. He decided that his quest for death, as well as the subject of divinity and his attempt to recreate the vision of his poems, represented "a whole cycle of inspiration and dead end."[23] He was beginning to consider his work of the past three years as a "broken record."[24] In the poem that registers his disillusionment with his former spiritual path, "Ode: My 24th Year," Ginsberg claims that he is giving up his attempts to record the

31

experience of Eternity; instead, he will try to accept living in the world of ordinary men. (It is interesting to note that although the poem is an ode to his twenty-fourth birthday, it wasn't put aside until after he was twenty-five, sometime in 1951, when he finally decided to leave it unfinished and dated "1950–1951.")

> No return when thought's completed;
> let that ghost's last gaze go cheated;
> I may waste my days no more
> pining in spirituall warre.[25]

Though he is still using an Elizabethan voice, "spirituall warre," he is abandoning the classic mystical path of embracing death in order to be taken into the bosom of eternal light. He is claiming that "the visionary gleam" is leading him nowhere, that "here is no Eden,"[26] and that he doesn't want to "waste my days" any longer.

***

The end of this phase in Ginsberg's poetics came when he received several of his poems back from William Carlos Williams with a note saying: "In this mode perfection is basic."[27] He held Williams in such awe that the gentle but firm reply to his poems by the elder poet was something of a disappointment. Though he himself knew that his poems to this point were imitative and somewhat awkward in their form and style, Williams' advice was the final push he needed to begin a new direction. He started thinking about his visions from a different point of view. After all, hadn't his looking at the cornices of the apartment building and noticing the unusual quality of the sky been the high points of the vision that accompanied his reading of "Ah! Sunflower"? Hadn't he experienced the sense of eternity he was constantly seeking by looking at a natural object, by observing the detail of craftsmanship in the bricks and cornices?

Ginsberg began to understand that the supernatural urge he had tried to convey in his poetry wasn't the real message of his visions. The great realization at that time had been "This

32

existence is it!" He hadn't been selected by Blake, nor had he been self-chosen, as a mystic to yearn after an incorporeal divinity or to be always moaning for union with the eternal. The "Sunflower" vision was an awakening into a deeper, more real, quotidian world. He realized this was what Williams was trying to tell him; Williams was an example of a poet creating a sense of the eternal by observing the details of everyday reality:

> So around that time, '50, '51, I ran into William Carlos Williams, so naturally the same thought [i.e., noticing detail] came to me, was Williams living, actually living in eternity observing the detail of eternity, but refusing to point to it as eternity, refusing to talk about it in poetic terms, refusing to talk about it symbolically... just directly perceiving what was in front of him.[28]

Not only was he impressed by Williams' method, but it also occurred to him that Blake had meant the same thing in his demand that the poet must record the minute particulars of reality—whether it be the reality of imagination or of the everyday world. Ginsberg became aware that his previous poetry represented an attempt to portray the visions—not as experienced, detail after detail, as he would in later poems, but always in a symbolic fashion, as in the manner of his predecessors. Thus Ginsberg was faced with the problem of starting all over again:

> ...thinking that, o.k., I can't make it by juggling symbolic language, referring to roses, light, spiritual wars, ineffable visions, so the only thing I can do is attempt to describe what I actually see, or actually saw, to pay attention to detail. To pay attention to minute particulars...[29]

This kind of careful attention duplicated the formula of his vision, when he noticed "in every corner where I looked evidence of a living hand, even in the bricks, in the arrangement of each brick."[30]

Another incident occurred about this time that reinforced his decision to write without literary trappings or symbolic abstractions. It had to do with the notebooks which Ginsberg used for jottings, sketches with words of things he saw. The notebooks were also used as preliminary drafts for his ambitious work, the serious poems he wrote between 1946 and 1951. Ginsberg had left all his notebooks at a friend's apartment for safe keeping while he was moving to Paterson, New Jersey. He moved partly to be closer to Williams, and partly to live cheaply with his family so he could devote himself to his writing. When he returned to claim his journals, he found his friend had read them. Ginsberg was somewhat embarrassed since the journals contained material about his private life that he hadn't yet confessed to anyone. He was curious, however, to hear his friend's reactions to their contents. His friend thought they were completely unreadable, too abstract and symbolic for coherent understanding. But, he told Ginsberg, there were one or two pages that he found absolutely absorbing. On these pages was a highly detailed description that Ginsberg had written in 1946 of two bricklayers having lunch. While in Denver, waiting for Cassady to arrive, he had notated, in a casual style with realistic detail and using natural language, exactly what the two bricklayers were doing. The friend who read the passage remarked that it was like "reading" a photograph. Ginsberg realized from this incident that it was this kind of presentation of detail, of recording minute particulars, that Williams and Blake insisted on as the formula for great art.

Ginsberg started rereading all his journals, which dated back to 1943, hoping to find other descriptions that reflected this eye for detail. He found another in an account of a dream he had had in 1947. He was astounded that all the time he had been writing rhymed verse, it was his matter-of-fact prose entries in his journal that actually captured the quality of perception and attention to detail which, as he saw, was the direction he had to take in order to be true to his understanding of existence as *it:*

> But I didn't take it as poetry, I took it as just writing in my journals, so I didn't, until several years later, arrange it into lines . . . [31]

At this point, he quite naturally started reading a lot of

Williams. He decided that Williams arranged his lines according to units of breath, that is, that the line ended with the natural breath stops of the voice. So he took the two entries in his journals that he considered accurate, literal renderings of minute detail in the real world, or vivid, actual accounts of a dream—without the usual rhetorical flourish—and arranged them into verse. He ended each line according to breath stops, as he assumed Williams did. The dream entry became the poem "In Society," later published in *Empty Mirror:*

> In Society
>
> I walked into the cocktail party
> room and found three or four queers
> talking together in queertalk.
> I tried to be friendly but heard
> myself talking to one in hiptalk.
> "I'm glad to see you," he said, and
> looked away. "Hmmm," I mused. The room
> was small and had a double-decker
> bed in it, and cooking apparatus:
> icebox, cabinet, toasters, stove...[32]

Ginsberg has characterized this poem as demonstrating the influence of both Blake and Williams:

> So those are literal renderings of actual material which, though less pretty than the rhymed poems I was writing, actually had more humor, more life in them, more detail, more minute particulars, less ideas, more things— "icebox, cabinet, toasters, stove"—*presenting* material, rather than recombining symbols...[33]

In Ginsberg's estimation, Blake's minute particulars were the equivalent of Williams' dictum "No ideas but in things." Ginsberg's new direction in poetry would reject the abstract and symbolic in favor of *"presenting* material," as he did in presenting the material of his dream, including every possible detail, such as conversations, observations of personalities, even down to the particulars of "icebox, cabinet, toasters, stove." Even in a dream record, which is not based on an ostensible perception of everyday reality, but rather on the reality of the mind itself, Ginsberg is after the "literal renderings of actual material"—in the same way as Blake was faithful to portraying the actual material of his visions, *while he experienced them*. In fact, Blake claimed that he wrote in a trance, and that the only artistry involved was that of not interfering with the original impulse.

The other poem that Ginsberg took from his prose journals became "The Bricklayer's Lunch Hour":

> Two bricklayers are setting the walls
> of a cellar in a new dug out path
> of dirt behind an old house of wood
> with brown gables grown over with ivy
> on a shady street in Denver. It is noon
> and one of them wanders off. The young
> subordinate bricklayer sits idly for a
> few minutes after eating a sandwich
> and throwing away the paper bag . . .[34]

He is simply describing exactly what he saw looking out of a window from his room in Denver. The poem is "a little notation on whatever completely photographic, instamatic sensory detail could be seen from a window."[35] As in "In Society," Ginsberg arranged the prose into verse lines where the breath ends, according to how they might be spoken.

Ginsberg continued to work in this new direction. He recognized that he couldn't rely on his prose journals for all his poetry. Somewhat unsure of himself, because the experiments were so radically different from his previous ones, he had a difficult time, at first, writing in his new style. However, one night after smoking a little marijuana, he made a short notation in his workbook, which he immediately recognized as the kind of verse he wanted. It is titled "Marijuana Notation":

> How sick I am!
> that thought
> always comes to me
> with horror.
> Is it this strange
> for everybody?[36]

He realized what he had been denying in his previous poetry:

> It took a little grass to make me realize I had been ignoring
> everyday perceptions, the more familiar perceptions ...
> here's a shift of diction and of approach to poetry that's
> more realistic—I'm still daydreaming, still talking about
> my own thoughts, but at least about it in a normal tone of
> voice that you can understand.[37]

By this time Ginsberg had been seeing Williams regularly. Williams kept telling him to write in a natural language, the language of the streets. He had written down a phrase of one of his patients to show Ginsberg exactly what he meant: "I'll kick yuh eye."[38] Williams told him that the metrical poetry he had seen of Ginsberg's had no relationship to that kind of real world "poetry." Ginsberg was very impressed. He realized that Williams didn't write according to any received, fixed rules, at least in terms of diction and syntax. Instead he "was taking rhythms directly from his own voice" and "listening to the rhythms he heard around him."[39]

With this realization about rhythms and voice, coupled with the notion of using the "raw materials" of experience, Ginsberg had made a major discovery about the poetry he was writing and the poetry he would write from that period on. This change is summed up in his analysis of "Marijuana Notation" quoted above: "a shift of diction and of approach to poetry that's more realistic..."[40] The shift in diction was from a literary, often Elizabethan rhetoric to his own natural voice and the rhythms of American speech that he heard around him. It was a logical consequence of his visionary formula that *"This existence is it."* In other words, he was accepting his own voice, the voice of this existence now, instead of repeating somebody else's rhythms, as he had been doing. The poetic notations in his journals all had this quality of natural, unaffected, everyday language.

Ginsberg had learned not only to speak in his own voice, but also to "make use of my own life, my own occasions."[41] He would approach poetry with an eye and ear for the real, celebrating this existence by rendering, as literally as possible,

37

the raw materials of reality. The importance of these two discoveries cannot be overstated. Ginsberg's decision to stop writing poems about a Supreme Reality, with, as he put it, "a capital S & R,"[42] was the beginning of a new phase that eventually led to "Howl" and "Kaddish"—both poems dedicated to the presentation of raw material and written in a natural voice. He was convinced that the eternal reality he had sought before could be realized by concentrating on the details of everyday existence, as he had experienced it while looking at the cornices and at the sky during his original visions. He had to reject his experiment in recording cosmic consciousness by trying to present himself as a "divine Blakean angel" and by conjuring up symbolic realities through abstractions and unnatural, archaic language. He must accept this existence as it is, be willing to accept himself, and record reality as perceived, instead of forcing a "visionary gleam":

> It was just the willingness to be that nowhere man, nowhere self, to be myself really, the humor involved in being that, rather than being a divine Blakean angel. I think that finally makes it possible to stand firmly on the ground in poems like this ["Bricklayer's Lunch Hour," etc.] and then begin constructing out of that reality, "I saw the best minds of my generation destroyed by madness."[43]

Ginsberg was encouraged in his new sense of writing by his mentor Williams and by his friend Kerouac. When he sent Williams some of the poems in his new style, Williams sent him back a note saying "Ah, this it it!"[44] He showed Kerouac, who had just completed *The Town and the City*, the poem "Marijuana Notation." Kerouac praised the last stanza, claiming the method was exactly like his own—writing down the mental picture. This observation was not only favorable but extremely accurate. The idea of literal rendering was very much the prose writer's notion of making a pencil sketch, as in Ginsberg's last stanza:

It is December
almost, they are singing
Christmas carols

                    in front of the department
                    stores down the block on
                    Fourteenth Street.[45]

This new method of Ginsberg's paralleled the method of
perception he had had when he looked out of his Harlem
apartment window and saw the "living blue hand of the sky"
and the "cosmic intelligence" of the workman's craftsmanship
in the cornices of the apartment building across the way.
Though at the writing of "Marijuana Notation" he wasn't
experiencing the same sense of heightened awareness as a few
years earlier, he did feel some of that glow or awe because of the
marijuana he had been smoking. In the late 1950's, Ginsberg
would make use of drugs in an attempts to regain this sense of
cosmic perception. For the time being, however, he was happy
to have at last completed an experiment in his study of
consciousness that had produced a notation sufficiently
grounded in the reality of daily living that both Williams and
Kerouac could praise it.

    In fact, the more writing Ginsberg did after this period, the
more committed he became to these two essential qualities of
his poetry: the natural voice and the literal rendering of the raw
materials. In "Howl" he would learn to combine these discoveries with others he would later master—all still stemming
from his Blake visions. In addition, enhancing this preoccupation with the details of existence, he would incorporate into his
poetry some of the methods of rendering reality discovered by
Cezanne, whom he had studied briefly in 1948. In "Kaddish,"
Ginsberg would use the method of presenting raw material as a
cataloque of epiphanous detail in relating the story of his and
his mother's life. In the book that followed, *Reality
Sandwiches*, Ginsberg humorously characterized the style of
the poems in that volume, as well as of others, in the short
poem "On Burroughs' Work," dated San Jose, 1954:

                The method must be purest meat
                and no symbolic dressing
                actual visions & actual prisons
                as seen then and now.[46]

39

Ginsberg wanted to make it clear that he had abandoned "symbolic dressing." Instead, he was dedicated to actual visions coming out of the clear and precise perception of reality, even though the reality might be as horrendous as he portrayed it in so many of the poems written after 1948.

His recently published work, the epic *The Fall of America*, is, in effect, a tribute to these two techniques, discovered after his initial misdirection, both of which he has continued to use since then. The poem describes Ginsberg riding around the U.S. in a Volkswagen bus, presenting a mental picture of America during the Vietnam War, as seen through the windshield of his bus. To ensure that he is using the natural voice, he tape-recorded most of the poems, using the click of the recorder to indicate when he paused, thus ensuring a precision of breath-stops that parallel line endings. He also included all the detail he could, with the added speed of talking, rather than writing with pen or pencil or typewriter. The following are a few lines, chosen at random, to underscore the extent to which the methods have become a natural part of his poetics:

> Grey water tanks in Grey mist,
> grey robot
> towers carrying wires thru Bayonne's
> smog, silver
> domes, green chinaworks steaming,
> Christmas's leftover lights hanging
> from a smokestack—
> Monotone grey highway into the grey West—[47]

The intense preoccupation with detail, the natural voice— Ginsberg had remained faithful to his early experiments. This method of literal rendering is the same as had been cautiously explored in the original experiments, "The Bricklayer's Lunch Hour" and "In Society." His dedication to the vision of "Ah! Sunflower" and to the lesson that "This existence is *it*" has become the cornerstone of his poetry and poetics, founded on the certainty that by studying the details of reality and communicating them with an absolute naturalness, one's consciousness may attain a glimpse of the infinite:

> In other words, the only way I could actually communicate
> the sense of eternity that I had, or might have, or wanted to
> have, was through concrete particular detail, grounding
> my mind, like taking the opposite direction of the
> apocalyptic light-hunger poetry that I'd been churning out
> before, taking exactly the opposite direction by turning
> around to face everyday universe, be human.[48]

Ginsberg had realized that in order to stay true to Blake and the
vision of "Ah! Sunflower," he would have to discover the
infinite in the real world; or as Blake puts it in *The Marriage of
Heaven and Hell:*

> If the doors of perception were cleansed
> everything would appear to man as it is,
> infinite.[49]

III

The Vision of Doom and Death

> *the second Vision—the Worm whose love*
> *is death . . .*
> *and because I am not now in*
> *a state of Vision*
> *and I despair age 34 attaining that*
> *moment again*
> *I defy my own consciousness*
> *in words*
> *because going to die I*
> *have nothing to fear from this reality . . .*
>
> —Ginsberg, unpublished poem,
> August 13, 1961[1]

Ginsberg's vision of Blake's "The Sick Rose" catalyzed in him a sense of his own death and the "doom of the universe," that would eventually have far-reaching effects on his life, poetry, and poetics. The vision of "the Worm whose love / is death" was a kind of instruction from Blake, Ginsberg believed, that demanded he face his own end, as well as the doom of everyone and everything around him:

I thought the instructions, Blake's instructions, meant delve right into the terror, cultivate the terror, get right into it, get right into death. I said, die, drop dead. So I thought for many years my obligation was to annihilate my ordinary consciousness by death. You know, to get rid of my ordinary consciousness and expand my consciousness; I thought the path was through the Gates of Wrath.[2]

His obligation to void ordinary consciousness would result in the major thematic quest of over half his poetry from 1948–63, and of much of it thereafter. He would explore not only his own concern with bodily and spiritual death, but also the "inevitable beauty of doom" inherent in modern culture and civilization. He understood Blake's command that in order really to "cleanse the doors of perception" and to achieve a vision of eternity in the world as it is, he must explore the minute particulars of reality by eliminating habitual modes of perception. To do this, Ginsberg systematically experimented with every possible form of consciousness, from mystical illumination to the horrors of psychedelic hallucination, from those induced by political and sexual experiments to the practice of mantra chanting and various forms of meditation. He would invent a unique approach to rhythm and imagery in his poetry that would allow him to express his new sense of eternity intersecting time. Even his method of composition, the spontaneous approach to writing, was primarily initiated by his vision of doom and death. It was an awesome vision: Blake's voice chanting "The Sick Rose" made Ginsberg face his own "death and also the death of being itself."[3] It left him with an unalterable certainty of the doom of the universe. This vision was an untutored enlightenment, a Zen-like sense of satori. In fact, Ginsberg himself has characterized Blake's poem as a Zen koan, with Blake as a Buddhist monk inducing the *sunyatta* ("fearless void") mind with his

> ...magic formula statement in rhyme and rhythm, that if heard in the inner ear, would deliver you beyond the universe.[4]

Ginsberg's exploration of doom began in the second poem

he wrote after his visionary seizures, the sonnet "Woe unto thee, Manhattan, woe to thee." Since he had nothing to fear in life, Ginsberg attacked Western culture, somewhat in the manner of the old Hebrew prophets warning of the fall of Babylon:

> Repent, Chicagos, O repent; ah, me!
> Los Angeles, now thou are gone so wild,
> I think thou are still mighty, yet shall be,
> As the earth shook, and San Francisco fell . . .[5]

This quotation helps to clarify the meaning of this thematic preoccupation. The more Ginsberg "clamped his eyes" on reality, particularly from 1952, after he had renounced the unreality of the supreme visions, the more he was faced with the atomic, self-destructive mania of Western civilization. His obligation was not only to expose the horrors, but to delve into the terror as much as he could, without fear of the consequences. As a result, scores of poems would have as their motif Ginsberg's revelations about the "tomb of souls"[6] that Western civilization has become, a culture "so much like Hell."[7]

Several poems in *Empty Mirror* explore the same theme, not as forcefully as in the "Woe unto thee . . ." sonnet, nor as dramatically as would be the case in "Howl" and later poems, but in a frightening fashion that makes it clear he is not dismissing the realities of America in the twentieth century. "A Meaningless Institution" is a prophetic dream of Ginsberg's finding himself in a mental hospital, months before he actually committed himself to psychiatric care. It is a desolate picture of Ginsberg totally destroyed by society, in a state of complete hopelessness wandering "off down empty corridors / in search of a toilet."[8] The theme recurs again in "I have increased power . . ." with a last stanza that perfectly characterizes his awareness of the dark path that one must travel beyond the Gates of Wrath:

> "How often have I
> had occasion to see
> existence display
> the affectations
> of a bloodthirsty
> negro homosexual."[9]

He is quoting his friend and fellow hospital patient Carl Solomon, whose perceptions of doom also echo through much of "Howl."

Before the ultimate poems of doom—"Howl" and "Kaddish"—Ginsberg explored the theme in other poems. In "Paterson," which is also in the volume *Empty Mirror*, Ginsberg announces he is giving up participation in society with its "visions of money." Instead, he vows he would rather go crazy "with a mouthful of shit" than be part of a culture so entrenched in repression. He announces that he will try to destroy America's "vision of electricity and daylight" and will dance and scream "in praise of Eternity annihilating the sidewalk, annihilating reality."[10] His vow to annihilate ordinary consciousness—a vow he took after the vision of "The Sick Rose"—has become forthright and dramatic by 1949, when "Paterson" was written.

This theme of renouncing American bourgeois values is repeated once again in the collection of poems *Reality Sandwiches*. Many of the poems in this book, his third published volume, predate "Howl" by two to three years. The first poem, "My Alba," renounces the wasted life he, and everyone else, has spent being acceptable citizens. He bemoans the loss of five years of his life working within a culture dedicated to deceiving the people with its "vast conspiracies."[11] The American doom appears in various images throughout the book, as in "Siesta in Xbalba" ("There is a god / dying in America . . ."[12]) and even in the sensual "Love Poem on Theme by Whitman," in which he alludes to "the inhabitants who roam unsatisfied in the night, / nude ghosts seeking each other out in the silence."[13] Of course, by the time Ginsberg began writing "Howl" in 1955, his famous announcement of doom and destruction had these and many other poems behind it. However, with the exception of some of the imagery and rhythmic power of the earlier "Paterson," "Howl" was indeed a surprise to many, and a threat to many more. With lines like

> who bit detectives in the neck and shrieked
> with delight in police cars for committing
> no crime but their own wild cooking

> pederasty and intoxication,
> who howled on their knees in the subway and
>   were dragged off the roof waving genitals
>   and manuscripts
> who let themselves be fucked in the ass by
>   saintly motorcyclists, and screamed for joy . . .[14]

Ginsberg had fully realized his quest to get right into the terror. The individual, victimized by the repression, fear, and violence that so permeates Western culture, had surfaced as one of Ginsberg's major themes. It would be repeated in various ways in "Kaddish," where his own mother is seen as a victim of political doom and paranoia; in "America," a satiric treatment of an America where "everyday somebody goes on trial for murder;"[15] in "Europe! Europe!," a brutal condemnation in which he hopes for an end to "death the cities" and "war the cities;"[16] and in various poems throughout Ginsberg's published work, including the final, ruthless description of doom in the poems that make up his epic on war, *The Fall of America*.

***

Ginsberg's death theme often goes hand-in-hand with the doom motif, though there are several poems that deal solely with his fascination with bodily death. Yet, before showing how his preoccupation with his death eventually merged with his quest to define the individual's as well as America's doom, it will be helpful to establish some of the characteristics of his descriptions of death, for these descriptions are extraordinarily extensive.

The impact of his vision of "The Sick Rose" had convinced him that he should focus on death. In a letter (1948) to his professor, Mark Van Doren, he tried to explain in a desperate poem his sense of the obligation:

> Die, Die, the spirit cried
>   Without
> Die, Die
>   I cannot die
> Cry out, Cry out
>   I cannot cry.[17]

He thought that Blake's spirit was asking him to die; hence he must attend to the terror of death. His poem about the vision of "The Sick Rose" had been yet another attempt to deal with Blake's command to die. The following version, dated and signed "East Harlem 1948," was included in another letter to Van Doren, with an unfinished second stanza omitted from the version published in *The Gates of Wrath:*

> On Reading Wm Blake's Poem "The Sick Rose"
>
> Rose of spirit, rose of light,
> Flower whereof all will tell,
> Is this the weak vision of my sight
> A fashion of the prideful spell
> Mystic charm and magic bright
> O judgement of fire and of fright?
>
> Rose I named thee afterward,
> In homage to the gardener
> Of my thought in his own world;
> But who named the terror
> [   ] still heard what Blake heard
> Or not be blinded in his mirror?
>
> What everlasting force confounded
> In its being, like some human
> Spirit shrunken in a bounded
> Immortality, what Blossom
> Inward gathers us, astounded?
> Is this the sickness that is doom?[18]

The poem is difficult to penetrate because of the highly symbolic style Ginsberg was using at the time. However, it is plain that the "terror" and the "fashion of the prideful spell" are allusions to St. John of the Cross, who warns the spiritual seeker that the painful realization which visionaries often have may completely overwhelm the aspirant. Ginsberg's vision of death consists of a horrible, secret knowledge that, in the manner of Blake's poem "The Lamb," makes him doubt the force which condemns man to a life bounded by mortality. Nevertheless, there is complete identification with the decaying rose blossoms, gnawed by the "Worm whose love is death."[19]

There are several poems in *The Gates of Wrath* that explore Ginsberg's preoccupation with death, including "A Very Dove," "Do We Understand Each Other?," "The Voice of Rock," "Psalm," "A Dream," and "In Memoriam." The list could include several others if the reader interpreted as allusions to death many of the highly abstruse images such as "the haggard gate ghost, hanging in the door," from "Please Open the Window and Let Me In," or "I dream that I have burning hair," from "The Shrouded Stranger." The following quotations from some of the poems in the list will give an idea of the intense focus on death and its terrors that possessed Ginsberg, not only in the few years after his visions, but, as we shall see, throughout the fifties and well into the sixties:

> A city where my soul
> Visited its vast
> Passage of the dead
>
> —"Do We Understand Each Other?"

> ...for what he knows and I have known
> is like a crystal lost in stone,
> hidden in skin and buried down
> blind as the vision of the dead.
>
> —"The Voice of Rock"

> All my youth, and Dead and Beauty cry,
> Like horns and motors from a ship afar,
> Half heard, an echo in the sea beneath,
> And Death and Beauty beckon in the dawn,
> A presage of the world of whitening shadows
> As another pale memorial.
>
> —"Psalm"

> I stared in phantom-attic dark
> At such radiant shapes of gloom,
> I thought my fancy and mind's lark
> So cried for Death that He had come.
>
> —"A Dream"

> ...while the man of the apocalypse
> shall with his wrath lay ever wed

until the sexless womb bear love,
and the grave be weary of the dead,

tragical master broken down
into a self embodied tomb,
blinded by the sight of death,
and woven in the darkened loom
> —"In Memoriam"

It becomes apparent from these examples that Ginsberg actually was trying to annihilate his consciousness by getting "right into death"—as often as he could, exploring the terror almost to the point where he "So cried for Death that He had come."

This intense desire was by no means a lingering shadow of his vision cast only over his early poems. The quest for death is a prevalent theme in his poems of the fifties and early sixties. It is evident in the titles of his new-styled verse collected in *Empty Mirror:* "In Death, Cannot Reach What is Most Near," "This is About Death," and "I Have Increased Power / over knowledge of death." Several of the poems written after these, collected in *Reality Sandwiches* and in *Howl and Other Poems,* also reflect Ginsberg's strange fascination. "Funny Death" (1959) and the superb dream vision about his dead friend, Joan Burroughs, "Dream Record" (June, 1955), show that during the mid- and late-fifties Ginsberg was still writing poems on this theme. Of course, his great lament for his dead mother, "Kaddish," is a long meditative account of the life and painful death of a woman dominated by paranoid flashes of people trying to kill her. However, it is less obvious that the book as a whole is conceived as an entire volume centered around poems on death, with a line from "Mescaline" characterizing the awful quest after annihilation:

> What happens when the death gong hits rotting
> ginsberg on the head[20]

"Mescaline," written in New York (1959), begins a series of five poems in which Ginsberg explores his terror of death under the influence of various psychedelic drugs, including mescaline, LSD, and a powerful "Amazon spiritual potion"[21] called Ayahuasca. The point of the experiments, as Ginsberg explains at the end of the book, is to follow Blake's command to "cleanse the doors of perception." These drug-induced meditations come at the end of a book in which he has already written about the death of his mother ("Kaddish"), the death of his aunt ("To Aunt Rose"), the suicide of the poet Vachel Lindsay ("To Lindsay"), a visit to the grave of Apollinaire ("At Apollinaire's Grave"), a poem about his own haunting death quest ("The Lion for Real"), a crazy spiritual in which he claims that he "wants to die give up go mad break through into Eternity" ("Ignu"), and a poem on the Artaud theme of Van Gogh killed by a ruthless society ("Death to Van Gogh's Ear"). These, and others, all explore the theme of death as a means of altering consciousness and of achieving the break-through into Eternity.

The interesting question remains whether Ginsberg achieved what he set out to accomplish. Did he find his sense of Eternity by jettisoning his ordinary consciousness and by exploring the doom-ruled reality of Western civilization, while also facing as honestly as he could the fact of his own bodily death? It is certain that by the time he began writing in his new style of prose-verse (prose, that is, with the rhythmic recurrences of verse, with minute attention to detail, and with the cadences of the natural voice), he had begun to understand that society was largely responsible for a death worse than natural decay—the death of the spirit, the soul, the intellect. The theme of bodily death and spiritual death, brought on by a culture bent on "visions of money,"[22] began first to appear in his poems as a timid compassion for the despairing situation of Blacks, as in the early "A Poem on America." Then, by the time he wrote "Paterson," the themes of doom and death had merged into a blazing attack on capitalism and its all-powerful bureaucracies. By confronting the two themes simultaneously, Ginsberg enabled himself to achieve the cleansing of his perception that he had sought. This combination of death and doom became the pattern in subsequent poems such as

50

"Howl," "Sunflower Sutra," and "Kaddish."

The first line of "Paterson" exemplifies the kind of flight against doom-by-culture that Ginsberg began in the sophomoric "Woe unto thee, Manhattan..." and carried on in so many later poems:

> What do I want in these rooms papered with
>   visions of money?
> How much can I make by cutting my hair? If
>   I put new heels on my shoes,
> bathe my body reeking of masturbation and sweat
>   layer upon layer of excrement
> dried in employment bureaus, magazine hallways,
>   statistical cubicles, factory stairways...[23]

The poems that achieve a vision of Eternity by combining the death and doom themes usually begin with a devastating attack on the doom-oriented society that causes so many spiritual and bodily deaths. This is the design of "Paterson" in the opening lines quoted above. Ginsberg begins with an attack on capitalism, and then renounces middle-class adaptability by ridiculing the compromises necessary to succeed in such a society. He proclaims war on "old clerks," who destroy creativity and vent their frustration on their employees because of their obsession with money and power.

In the next stanza, Ginsberg swears he'd rather confront death head-on than accept a place in that "harridan vision of electricity."[24] After "annihilating the sidewalk, annihilating reality,"[25] he achieves a sense of self "screaming and dancing in praise of Eternity."[26] The eternity, however, is not the sublime, beautiful vision of light achieved after hearing Blake singing "Ah! Sunflower." Instead, it is the vision of "The Sick Rose," in which he experienced the certainty of the death and the doom of being itself:

> screaming and dancing against the orchestra in
>   the destructible ballroom of the world
> blood streaming from my belly and shoulders
> flooding the city with its hideous ecstasy,
>   rolling over the pavements and highways

51

> by the bayoux and forests and derricks leaving
>   my flesh and my bones hanging on the trees.[27]

Death and doom have merged in a transcendental vision. Habitual perception is annihilated. The vision is of eternity and stems from the Buddhist sword of fire, eliminating everything, including self.

Yet, in several poems written a few years later, Ginsberg would achieve the blissful, all-accepting consciousness of light by combining the death and doom themes, to emerge with a vision of eternity that is full of cosmic awe. The reader will remember that "Howl" begins with an attack on a society that destroys the best minds of each generation by madness. It then continues with one of the most eventful and frightening visions of the reality of doom to be found in our literature. But the "Footnote to Howl" completes the pattern first seen in "Paterson." It is a trance-inducing vision of life so mystical that the consciousness achieved is indeed the result of an annihilation of ordinary consciousness and an entrance into a sense of the holy—a cosmic awareness:

> Holy! Holy! Holy! Holy! Holy! Holy! Holy!
>   Holy! Holy! Holy! Holy! Holy! Holy! Holy!
>   Holy! Holy!
> The world is holy! The soul is holy! The skin
>   is holy! The tongue and cock and hand and
>   asshole holy!
> Everything is holy! everybody's holy!
>   everywhere is holy! everyday is eternity!
>   Everyman's an angel![28]

A devastating confrontation with doom and death leads to a new consciousness of total acceptance, a glimpse of the cosmic that he has seen.

"Kaddish" is the other major poem to follow the pattern of "Paterson" and "Howl." After the beautiful and painful description of the death of his mother, and of the suffering she endured—real or imagined—from a society that persecuted her for her political philosophy, finally incarcerating her after she had been reduced to paranoid hallucinations, Ginsberg ends the poem with a vision of blessedness and a feeling of eternity:

> Caw caw caw crows shriek in the white sun over grave
>   stones in Long Island
> Lord Lord Lord Naomi underneath this grass
>   my halflife and my own as hers
> caw caw my eye be buried in the same Ground where
> I stand an Angel
> Lord Lord great Eye that stares on All and moves
>   in a black cloud...
>
> caw caw all years my birth a dream caw caw New
>   York the bus the broken shoe the vast high school
>   caw caw all Visions of the Lord
> Lord Lord caw caw Lord Lord Lord caw caw Lord.[29]

Here is a final lament that records the transcendental, a celebration of the spirit of the universe, of the Lord, as well as of the common grass. It parallels the consciousness of bliss in the section of "Kaddish" titled "HYMMNN":

> Magnified Lauded Exalted the Name of the Holy
>   One Blessed is He!
> In the house in Newark Blessed is He! In the
>   madhouse Blessed is He! In the house of Death
>   Blessed is He![30]

Once again Ginsberg confronts doom ("In the madhouse...") and death ("In the house of Death Blessed is He!"). The result is a state of awareness that actually does embody a vision of Eternity, an eternity that is so awesome it transcends normal reason and common sense. He has pursued Blake's instructions to their logical goal.

The best example of Ginsberg's visionary quest, ending in a vision of Eternity, is "Sunflower Sutra." The poem specifically refers to his Blake experience and also describes his perceptions of a dying sunflower, dying because the soot and grime of a thoughtless, mechanical society have weighed so heavily upon it. This description of the sunflower—a projection of Ginsberg's own self, "my sunflower O my soul"—is a description of the suffering he has endured at the hands of a culture steeped in doom and death:

> and those bleak thoughts of death and dusty loveless
> eyes and ends and withered roots below,
> in the home-pile of sand and sawdust, rubber
> dollar bills, skin of machinery, the guts and
> innards of the weeping coughing car, the
> empty lonely tincans with their rusty tongues
> alack, what more could I name, the smoked
> ashes of some cock cigar, the cunts of
> wheelbarrows and the milky breasts of cars,
> wornout asses out of chairs & sphincters of
> dynamos—all these
> entangled in your mummied roots—and you there
> standing before me in the sunset, all your
> glory in your form![31]

And again, in the midst of a bleak death caused by the grime of a "mad locomotive," which for him symbolized society, Ginsberg realizes, in the manner of "The Sick Rose," another vision of Eternity. It is the pattern established in the early poem "Paterson":

> —We're not our skin of grime, we're not our
> dread bleak dusty imageless locomotive, we're
> all beautiful golden sunflowers inside, we're
> blessed by our own seed & golden hairy naked
> accomplishment-bodies growing into mad black
> formal sunflowers in the sunset, spied on by
> our eyes under the shadow of the mad locomotive
> riverbank sunset Frisco hilly tincan evening
> sitdown vision.[32]

The height of vision, the "inevitable beauty of doom" was what Ginsberg had experienced when hearing Blake's voice seven years earlier. Ginsberg transcends the forces of our society by coming forth with a vision of Eternity that claims we are all spirits, all angels, "all beautiful golden sunflowers inside."[33]

The union of Ginsberg's two themes of death and doom marked the culmination of his experiments with consciousness. But his experiments were to continue. In the late fifties, guided by his use of mescaline, LSD, aether, and other drugs, he

54

would re-examine his fascination with death. In the resulting poems, such as "Aether," "Lysergic Acid," and "Magic Psalm," the drug visions ultimately leave him fearful and confused. The path through the Gates of Wrath is so much a defiance of everyday reality that he is overwhelmed. However, at this point it is necessary to consider the formative influence of his quest for annihilation on his writing techniques, and specifically on his frequent abandonment of a rational approach to writing, and on a theory of composition dubbed the spontaneous method of composition, or, as he would later call it in 1974, "First Thought, Best Thought."

***

Ginsberg's vow to annihilate consciousness meant rejecting all preconditioning so as to be true to the spirit of Blake. In technique, it meant learning how to get rid of a false literary voice and to rely instead on his natural breath patterns—his speaking voice. It meant throwing out all invented literary situations, such as ideas about his vision modeled on other visions. It meant writing simply from the immediacy of his own reality. But the attempt to realize, unrestrictedly, a certain state of consciousness also meant learning how to write without literary crutches, without that sense of literary craft that told him to cross out one phrase and insert another—even though the original phrase may have been straight from the depths of consciousness. Ginsberg, from his vision of "The Sick Rose," had a tremendous fear of tampering with the natural impulses of his consciousness. To be true to Blake's instructions, he must, without interference, spontaneously write whatever came from his mind. He realized that his vow to Blake entailed breaking down preconceptions, facing the universe with a sense of fearlessness and absolute honesty. He realized that the stakes were too high for any concessions to be made to literary conditioning or feeling of cultural propriety. Therefore, he swore he would always write spontaneously, true to those impulses by which, he knew, glimpses of the truths of eternity were granted:

> . . .for that reason [the relentless power of doom and the realization of death] all loves, poetics, and politics and intellectual life and literary scenes and all travels or stay-home years are by me pursued as much spontaneously without plan, without restrictive regulation of Rules and Rights and Wrongs and Final Judgements, without fixed ideas—as much as possible.[34]

The spontaneous method of composition came to him as a unique, courageous approach to creativity, a complete turnabout from the rational and contrived idea of art as a perfectly finished product. He would rely on "the immediate flash material from the mind as it came from the complete unconscious."[35] This would eliminate the popular notion of art-technique that demands revision, the draft after draft manipulation, that is so respected in Western culture. He was convinced that spontaneity insured an

> . . .introduction of courage and openness in the writing so that you'd realize you were already in eternity while you were living on earth.[36]

This approach reinforced Ginsberg's ideas about Blake and Plotinus and their insistence that true knowledge is intuitive. Indeed, Plotinus claimed that the intuitive approach was the highest state of cognition, something that is perfect in its own essence. Spontaneity also met the demands of Burroughs, who had been tutoring Ginsberg in Spenglerian philosophy and insisting that he respect "the irrational or unconscious properties of the soul."[37] The drive toward acceptance of this method culminated when his tutor-in-prosody and the originator of the idea of spontaneous writing, Jack Kerouac, read some of Ginsberg's early prose-into-poetry renderings from the journals. Kerouac was highly complimentary about the poem "Walking home at night":

> Walking home at night,
> reaching my own block
>   I saw the Port Authority
> Building hover over
>   the ghetto side
> of the street I tenement [*sic*]

56

> in company with obscure
> Bartlebys and Judes,
>   cadaverous men,
> shrouded men, soft white
> fleshed failures creeping
> in and out of rooms like
>   myself. Remembering
>   my attic, I reached
> my hands to my head and hissed
> "Oh, God how horrible!"[38]

Ginsberg had recorded, spontaneously, an actual experience of "mind thought or self thought or personal thought that is so accurate, like a little flash of oneself in a funny moment."[39] Kerouac thought the poem was absolutely true to life, amazingly the real Ginsberg, a true epiphany. He felt that Ginsberg had finally caught life as it is without any decoration or artificial literary motifs. Ginsberg, too, recognized that the poem was not only spontaneous, but true to the experience it sought to portray. It was written in the early 1950's, while he was living in Manhattan doing market research. Unlike most of his writing, which he worried over hour after hour, this piece was written in a few minutes in his journal and remained untouched after the initial entry. Ginsberg began to realize that spontaneity actually ensured truth because there wasn't any reason to change or camouflage anything.

It was about this time that Kerouac wrote down his rules for spontaneous composition. He was insisting that Ginsberg abandon his academic training that led him to compose over-written stanzas based on the notion of autonomous art forms. All previous literary techniques and preconceived forms were basically an avoidance of the truth, Kerouac told him. He encouraged Ginsberg to write more poems like "Walking home at night," because it was so unerringly real, because it had been written spontaneously, and because it showed a basic acceptance of the most difficult of truths—living for the here and now, while accepting whatever one is, or what one perceives:

> He bought it ... accepted the worst image instead of
> accepting an image of myself as an angel, accepting myself

57

> as a soft white fleshed failure creeping in and out of rooms
> like myself stuck, drab, "God, how horrible!"[40]

So Ginsberg took Kerouac's advice; he asked his friend for a copy of his rules for composition—later printed as the "Essentials of Spontaneous Prose"—and pinned it on a wall in front of him wherever he wrote. (Robert Duncan noticed the rules on the wall in Ginsberg's room in San Francisco during the composition of "Howl," and was so impressed by the notion of Kerouac's method that he asked Ginsberg for a copy.)

The spontaneous method of composition is aptly described by Ginsberg as

> Speak now, or ever hold your peace, write whatever comes to mind, adding vowels, adding alluvials, adding to the end of the sentence, and then rather than revising, if you have a new thought, go on to articulate it in the next sentence.[41]

Kerouac's own description of the method is similar. He calls it "Sketching language in undisturbed flow from the mind of personal secrets."[42] Like Ginsberg, he stresses no revision, urging the writer to throw away any preconceived idea of what to think and simply to write whatever is in the mind at the time of composition:

> Begin not from preconceived idea of what to say about image but from jewel center of interest in subject of image at moment of writing, and write outwards swimming in a sea of language to a peripheral release of exhaustion. Do not afterthink ... the best writing is always the most painful person wrung-out tossed from cradle warm protective mind—tap from yourself the song of yourself, *blow!—now!—your* way is your way—"good"—or "bad"—always honest, ("ludicrous"), spontaneous, "confessional," interesting, because not "crafted." Craft *is* craft.[43]

Kerouac is insisting that the writer abandon the popular notion of highly crafted writing that is self-conscious and based on a scientific precision with the artist in complete control. The notion of spontaneity works against this idea, trying to get below the conscious mind for the sake of honesty and the hope that free-association and exploration will produce hitherto unexpected truths or unrecognized rhythms and images. Early jazz musicians used a similar technique, and Kerouac uses the terminology of jazz. He speaks of blowing your own way, freely, openly, in long, deeply inspired mind-riffs, "*blowing* (as per jazz musician) on subject of image."[44]

Ginsberg also claims that spontaneity is a way of writing in lieu of the usual conception of crafted art. In fact, he ceased to accept the word "craft" as applied to his poetry, because it implies restrictions based on preconceived notions of what's "proper," what's expected. He remained firm in his conviction that a free-flowing exploration of consciousness is the most likely way to unveil a fresh vision of mind:

> Primary fact of my writing is that I don't have any craft and don't know what I'm doing. There is absolutely no art involved, in the context of the general use of the words *art* and *craft*. Such craft or art as there is, is in illuminating mental formations, and trying to observe the naked activity of my own mind. Then transcribing that activity down on paper. So the craft is being shrewd at flashlighting mental activity. Trapping the archangel of the soul, by accident, so to speak. The subject matter is the action of the mind.[45]

He believes that it is impossible to say what one has in mind by means of closed forms such as the sonnet; on the other hand, by abandoning all notions of craft, by going beyond the boundaries of convention, what's underneath, *inside* the mind, can be laid bare. Therefore, since the subject matter is actually no less than the movements of the mind itself,

> ...anything that the mind passes through is proper and shouldn't be revised out, almost anything that passes through the mind, anything with the exception of self-consciousness ... So you're making a graph of the movements of the mind, there is no point in revising it. Because you would obliterate the actual markings on the graph.[46]

No less a practical visionary than Gertrude Stein followed, in this respect, the same path.

Ginsberg believes that writing is not a rational act, that it is, primarily, spontaneous, based on a reliance on the intuitive qualities of mind. This is the method practiced by Zen haiku poets and calligraphers. Haiku writers, in Ginsberg's conception, aren't supposed to struggle for a perfect phrase or image, version after blue-penciled version. The haiku, like his own poetry, arises naturally, spontaneously, from the perception of the moment. It is an ability to write just the way you are. Spontaneity and intuitiveness are necessary and limitations are to be avoided, because consciousness itself knows no limitations. Ginsberg's vow to eliminate consciousness and his dedication to the intuitive and spontaneous method of writing have the same purpose: to explore the unknown without limitations. He believes that transcribing the deep, secret messages of the mind, as they actually appear in thought, may lead him to a new awareness:

> . . .to transcribe [thought] in a form most nearly representing its actual "occurrence" is my "method"—which requires the Skill of freedom of composition—and which will lead Poetry to the expression of the highest moments of mind-body-mystical illumination . . .[47]

An interesting feature of the spontaneous method is the handling of time during the act of composition. As Kerouac writes in his "Essentials," "Time [is] of the essence."[48] Ginsberg thought about this and decided that Kerouac meant that the length of the thought during composition dictated the length of the line. As he would later discover that the length of breath in vocalizing poetry could be a determining factor that governs the length of each line, he now realized that at the ending of each thought he could either end the line, or use a dash, to indicate that the thought was finished and that another was immediately forthcoming. In other words, the poem could be made a graph of the mind by the skillful arrangement of the lines, or units within the lines, to indicate thoughts beginning and thoughts ending. Thus, he could be absolutely faithful to consciousness in form as well as in spirit. The spontaneous method would become a form dictated by the duration of each thought. When a poem is organized in this fashion, not only is the line arrangement true to the mind, but the overall, finished poem becomes an example of the mind's structure. This is how Ginsberg would interpret Kerouac's insistence that one take the element of time into consideration. It is what Ginsberg means when he says, "Time of composition is the structure of the poem."[49]

An important aspect of this reliance on time to govern the structure of the lines and the overall form of the poem is that it enables the poet to concentrate most of his attention on the actual workings of the mind. Since form is nothing more than an extension of content, the poet is relieved of the exterior, somewhat unnatural concern over what the poem looks like. Instead, the attention is focused on the raw materials of deep thought, and the method of writing is trained almost exclusively on the exploration of consciousness. Ginsberg can attempt to

> ...arrive at a poetry that really means what it says, a poetry with a meaning which is identical with its form, with a rhythm identical with the arrangement of the words on the page, and the words on the page arranged identically with what you want to say and how you want to say it ...[50]

The act of writing becomes a form of meditation, a kind of writing that proposes "an absolute, almost Zen-like, complete absorption, attention to your consciousness, to the act of writing, to a focus of mind."[51]

What Ginsberg had already realized from his vision of "Ah! Sunflower" had been extended, with his incorporation of the spontaneous method, to include a dedication to the natural flow of thought. The mind itself would organize and control the actual form of his poems! And what of the Western concern for rational organization and logical coherence to tie things neatly together? Since the poem is usually written in one sitting, by one mind, with its own set of preoccupations and obsessions, the very nature of such composition gives the poem, oddly enough, the most rational organization possible—an organization based on the subject as it actually is. In other words, the method of writing itself ties the poem together. The beginning, middle, and end, which represents

61

basic Westen form, is present by the very nature of the mind making, unmaking, and finishing thoughts.

Ginsberg's transcription of the minute particulars of the mind, then, is the ultimate phenomenological perception, in Husserl's best sense. The essence of his spontaneous method of composition becomes: "How do we think?":

> In other words, this is like a form of Yoga: attempting to pronounce aloud the thoughts that are going through the head. But to do that you have to figure out where that . . . *how* the thoughts go through your head. Or do they go through as a series of words, or do they go through your head as full sentences or as phrases?[52]

By using the dash or line endings to score the thought, Ginsberg would solve part of the problem. Other solutions would come with his experiments in consciousness under the influence of drugs and with the incorporation of Cezanne's techniques of juxtaposition and parallelism. For the time being, in the early and mid-fifties, Ginsberg would explore his new method and come forth with some of the most original poems in the language: the "Moloch" section of "Howl," "Sunflower Sutra" (composition time: twenty minutes), and the "Proem" [*sic*] to "Kaddish." It was a way of writing that he would use as often as possible, accounting for well over two-thirds of his published poetry, most of his unpublished journals, and all of his recently published songs. Thus, Blake's voice chanting "The Sick Rose" had a tremendous impact on Ginsberg's poetics: in theme, the quests of doom and death; and in method, his use of Kerouac's theory of spontaneity. That chanting voice was an awesome vision, one that would haunt him for fifteen years, relentlessly forcing him to experiment with difficult and different modalities of consciousness in an attempt to create a poetry that not only truly means what it says, but says something seldom thought, much less imagined.

IV

The Heightened Awareness of a Prophet

Poet-prophet-friend on the side of love & the wild Good. That's the karma I wanted—to be a Saint.

—Ginsberg, early 1950's[1]

I am Thy prophet come home this world to scream an unbearable Name thru my 5 senses hideous sixth ...

—from "Magic Psalm," 1960[2]

As the world slowing draws to its doom dead ocean conclusion in the 2000th year, it gets harder and harder ... The poetic precedent for this situation is like Ezekiel and Jeremiah and the Hebrew prophets in the Bible who were warning Babylon against its downfall.

—Ginsberg, 1973[3]

During and after Ginsberg's other visionary experiences—particularly under the spell of Blake's poem

63

"The Little Girl Lost"—he felt as though he had participated in the total consciousness of the universe. The change in his ordinary state of mind allowed him to feel he was in the presence of a Creator, and that he was blessed with the ability to see into the truth of things, "a consciousness that was really seeing all heaven in a flower."[4] The visions in the bookstore, while walking around the Columbia campus, and even in his kitchen, convinced him that he had been chosen as a "spirit angel"—which, he thought, was a "terrible fucking situation to be confronted with."[5] He realized that his visionary experiences were not unlike the calling forth of the Hebrew prophets by their Creator, when He appeared to them in their visions. Ginsberg was beginning to realize that his role as a poet also entailed a kind of prophetic quest; his immediate problem, though, was how to make this plain to people without alarming them.

In time, Ginsberg would develop an identity of himself as a poet-prophet. It was what he called the "Messianic Thing," that he worked at over the years. But, at first, the overwhelming sense of his visions was so awesome, so frightening that he was worried it might scare others away, or that he would be attacked for communicating the awful truths of the surety of death and of universal doom, or even the blissful and startling perception of eternity:

> So there was that immediate danger. It's taken me all these years to manifest it and work it out in a way that's materially communicable to people. Without scaring them or me. Also movements of history and breaking down the civilization. To break down everybody's masks and roles sufficiently so that everybody has to face the universe and and the possibility of the sick rose coming true and the atom bomb. Which seems to be becoming more and more justified. So it was an *immediate Messianic Thing.*[6]

He would experiment in different poetic modes in order to recreate for his readers a "prophetic illuminative seizure":

> . . .the ambition is to write during a prophetic illuminative seizure. That's the idea: to be in such a state of complete

blissful consciousness that any language emanating from that state will strike a responsive chord of blissful consciousness from any other body into which the words enter and vibrate.[7]

Ginsberg's aim was to enlighten his readers by writing such miraculous poetry that it would cause them to experience a similar "cosmic awe" to that which Blake's poetry had caused in him. He began to think there could be no better purpose for his art:

> because I believe in it as Miracles
> and I wish to express thee a Miracle
>   at last, Man
> and create my miracle merely by
>   writing it down,
> Poetry is that secret formula for
>   miracles—
> No lesser purpose for my art...[8]

He considered his role of poet-prophet as part of the miraculous tradition of his creator, William Blake, who had caused miracles in Ginsberg's psyche by writing his prophecies down. In order to understand Ginsberg's prophetic quest, it is necessary first to consider what he thought the role of poet-prophet involved. Afterwards, I shall show how Ginsberg frequently alluded to this role in many of his poems from 1948 onward. This chapter will conclude with a discussion of the techniques he used in order to achieve his "Messianic Thing."

***

After his experience of hearing Blake's voice and the subsequent heightening of his awareness, Ginsberg spent a considerable amount of time trying to make sense of his visions in light of the role he had been selected by Blake to fulfill. He recognized that the Latin conception of the poet as *vates,* the prophetic seer, fitted his own identity as a divinely inspired poet who could now see below the surface of reality into the very essence of existence. He returned to his readings in Plato, particularly the *Ion* and *Phaedrus,* and applied to himself the description of the poet as divine madman able to glimpse the ultimate nature of things.

When Ginsberg started searching through Blake's writing for a model for his role as poet-prophet, he was startled by Blake's insistence that, ideally, "every man is a Prophet."[9] Blake thought of all great poetry as prophecy, and believed part of the role of the poet was to help his fellow men perceive the depths of reality. But an important distinction is implied in Blake's notion of prophecy, one that Ginsberg immediately recognized as important for himself. Blake's prophet is not a person who predicts the future; rather, the prophet sees deeper into the meaning of things. As the scholar S. Foster Damon points out, Blake's own poem-prophecies

> . . .were not prophecies in the conventional sense, as they were written after the facts; but they are prophecies in the poetic sense because they record the eternal formula for all revolutions.[10]

Blake himself said that prophets "never say, such a thing shall happen . . . A prophet is a Seer, not an Arbitrary Dictator"[11] of the future. Therefore, the reader should not be confused with the popular idea of a prophet as the magician, who can tell what's going to happen. Instead, the poet-prophet is a revealer of eternal truths, a seer—not the foreteller of the future.

Ginsberg's concept of himself as a poet-prophet is completely compatible with Blake's notion that prophecy is a formula for revolution; the revolution, in Blake's sense, was not primarily political, but a revolution of sensibility, of consciousness. Ginsberg adopted that notion of prophecy when he declared that his poetry was "a secret formula for miracles," dedicated to the "zapping of all consciousness."[12] Poetry dedicated to revolutionary truths was "not merely a sharing of human secrets," but ultimately

> . . .a sharing of non-human, the cosmic, universal archetypal knowledge of something beyond my own life.[13]

But Ginsberg's secret knowledge was unlike Blake's. Ginsberg's awareness was not of the blissful consciousness of a unified Man, but of the surety of impending disaster. His poetic

66

prophecy was more akin to that of the Old Testament prophets:

> The poetic precedent for this situation is like Ezekiel and
> Jeremiah and the Hebrew prophets in the Bible who were
> warning Bablyon against its downfall . . . They were talk-
> ing about the fall of a city, like Babylon, or the fall of a tribe,
> or cursing out the sins of a nation.[14]

Ginsberg felt that the kind of prophecies he must write weren't
unlike those written during the decadent and destructive times
of ancient Babylon. But, more than two thousand years later,
the situation had become even worse. With the ever-present
threat of the bomb, the death of the great lakes and oceans, and
the thoughtless pollution of the air, he realized that he couldn't
find a model that compared with the almost certain death, not
only of the body, but of the earth—indeed, of existence itself:

> But no poets have ever had to confront the *destruction of*
> *the entire world* like we have to . . . It's so incredible as a
> subject that you can't even go back to the biblical prophets
> for a model to say "Well, I think I'll write a poem like
> Jeremiah now . . ." not even Jeremiah had to confront a
> subject as immense as what I and you have to deal with,
> which is the end of the habitable human world. Or the
> millenial salvation of the human world. If we make it past
> 2000.[15]

It is the problem of conceiving poetic images so powerful
that they can measure up to the horrible reality that the
average person faces reading the morning newspaper. No
wonder Ginsberg would resolve to write a poetry that should,
ideally, be what he described as "a catalyst to visionary states
of being."[16] The poet as prophet had such a momentous task
that nothing short of a miracle could help him to heighten
awareness, not of what is going to happen, but of what is
actually happening now. He would try to create a sense of the
impending holocaust by making people see things as he saw
them, and making them share his belief in the urgency of
change. His prophetic role as a poet, then, included the
responsibility of saving humanity from certain extinction, of
turning people from a will to death, towards a will to a cleansed

perception of being. This was the task he felt his visions had awakened him to—the "Messianic Thing," the task of breaking down everybody's masks and roles so that people had to face the universe. They had to be made to realize there is no alternative but to seek enlightenment.

***

Ginsberg began alluding to his prophetic role in the poems as early as 1949. "Psalm" contains one extremely cryptic stanza that declares he has been chosen for his *vatic* role and is dedicated to the revolutionary miracles that will come from his art:

> A Bird of Paradise, the Nightingale
> I cried for not so long ago, the poet's
> Phoenix, and the erotic Swan
> Which descended and transfigured Time,
> And all but destroyed it, in the Dove
> I speak of now, is here, I saw it here
> The Miracle, which no man knows entire
> Nor I myself. But shadow is my prophet,
> I cast a shadow that surpasses me,
> And I write, shadow changes into bone,
> To say that still Word, the prophetic image
> Beyond our present strength of flesh to bear.[17]

He begins by listing birds that have represented spiritual quests in literature—the Nightingale (Death), the Phoenix (usually Rebirth), and even Yeats' "erotic Swan" (possibly regeneration)—declaring that he once yearned for them, as have most poets at one time or another. But, after his visions, he followed a different symbolic bird, the Dove—in the tradition of Christ's baptism, where a Dove descended as proof that the people's true prophet from God was on earth, come to reveal human secrets as well as cosmic, archetypal knowledge. Ginsberg was part of a miracle symbolized in the apparition of the Dove: [what] "I speak of now, is here, I saw it here." He is, in his early symbolic style, claiming that he is bringing prophetic images "Beyond our present strength to bear." The image of the Dove appears in several other of Ginsberg's early poems, and always alludes to his visionary experience and prophetic annointment—as in the obscure poem "A Very Dove." The Dove resurfaces in a poem in his new style of clear presentation and natural voice, "Psalm": "This is an eccentric document to be lost in a library and rediscovered when the Dove descends."[18] This symbol is most clearly defined in "Hymm," as the prophetic vision, "the very summa and dove of the unshrouding of finality's joy,"[19] where he also declares that the Dove is a visionary gleam, the "dreamy essences"[20] of the heart and eternity.

Also in "Psalm," Ginsberg declares that his poems—his "psalms"—are the result of a prophetic quest induced by "the working of the vision haunted mind,"[21] as in the tradition of other prophets, like Ezekiel or Jeremiah. In "After all, What Else Is There To Say," Ginsberg announces that "my poem itself"[22] is his way of telling the truth of prophecy. He says that all he does is wait for the prophetic spirit to enter him, cleansing his perception and heightening his awareness, as it had in Harlem:

> but to think to see, outside,
> in a tenement the walls
> of the universe itself
> I wait: wait till the sky
> appears as it is . . .[23]

By 1954, Ginsberg was outwardly characterizing his poetry as "primitive illuminations" and prophetic "apparitions,"[24] with the

> anterior image
> of divinity
> beckoning me out.[25]

In "Psalm III," written in Seattle in 1956, Ginsberg addresses his Creator, claiming that he will be true to his prophetic role and illuminate everyone, "Beginning with Skid Road."[26] ("Psalm III" is part of a series of poems on the theme of Ginsberg's prophetic quest. The first, the unnumbered "Psalm," was written in 1949; and the latest was written in the early 1960's and not yet collected in book form.)

69

The vow in "Psalm III" to save his fellow man, characteristic of Ginsberg's notion of himself as a "poet-prophet-friend,"[27] also parallels the Bodhisattva oath he took about this time, while studying Buddhism in Berkeley with Kerouac and Gary Snyder. A Bodhisattva is similar to a Hebrew prophet, in that he is an enlightened man who has achieved satori and vows to help others attain it. In fact, Ginsberg would later describe the Bodhisattva as a prophet whose task it is to save others:

> . . .the Bodhisattva is one who sets himself on the path of enlightenment, or perhaps glimpsed enlightenment, and now wants to incorporate it completely . . . anybody who is a Bodhisattva on the path is not allowed to go to Nirvana all by himself alone and disappear into eternity . . .[28]

His vow in "Psalm III" is his prophetic equivalent of the Bodhisattva's pledge: "Sentient beings are numberless, I vow to save them all":

> To God: to illuminate all men. Beginning with
>   Skid Road.
> Let Occidental and Washington be transformed
>   into a higher place, the plaza of eternity.[29]

By the late fifties Ginsberg had become quite frank about his identity as a poet-prophet. In a poem written while under the influence of LSD, he once again attained a vision of his Creator and eternity and felt reaffirmed in his commitment to help mankind attain true knowledge and a recognition of the eternal state:

> I see the gay Creator
> Bands rise up in anthem in the worlds
> Flags and Banners waving in transcendence
> One image in the end remains myriad-eyed in
>   Eternity
> This is the Work! This is the Knowledge!
> This is the End of Man![30]

Ginsberg's claim is that the work of a prophet is to help others achieve and accept a vision of Eternity, a consciousness that ultimately transcends the body and life. He is committed to "this knowledge," for it is the "Work!" of the poet-prophet.

In the poem that follows, "Magic Psalm," the second in a series of five drug poems that deal, in part, with his prophetic quest, Ginsberg declares that he is ready for the challenge, boasting that

> I am Thy prophet come home this world to scream
> an unbearable Name thru my 5 senses hideous
> sixth . . .[31]

He is announcing that he is prepared for the ultimate prophetic task, making people accept "the possibility of the sick rose coming true."[32] That possibility is Death, portrayed in "Magic Psalm" as his prophetic Dove: "The Ark-Dove with a bough of Death."[33] In this poem Ginsberg calls on his Creator to descend and aid him in his prophecy, admitting that he is afraid, but ready for the ultimate "disintegration of my mind":

> devour my brain One flow of endless consciousness,
> I'm scared of your promise must make scream
> my prayer in fear—[34]

The role of poet-prophet manifested itself in multiple ways in Ginsberg's poetry from 1948–63. "Howl" could easily be interpreted as a prophetic poem in the tradition of the Old Testament, since Ginsberg studied the rhythms of the Old Testament to achieve the hypnotic cadences of his masterpiece. Of course, many of his poems deal with the prophetic task of making the world conscious of its impending demise, as in "Howl," "Europe! Europe!," "Paterson," and in the series of lyrics that make up his ultimate poem in the Babylon-Jeremiah tradition, *The Fall of America*. The poet-prophet as a seer, penetrating beneath the surface of reality, is the theme of many of his drug poems, including "Aether," "The End," and "The Reply," in which Ginsberg makes it clear that his endeavor is to enlarge areas of consciousness. This was a serious responsibility, one that drove him to the borders of sanity and led to bouts of despair. At one point he thought his prophecies were going to be completely wasted because of the impending atomic doom:

> For instance, I begin to wonder what's the point of writing
> poems down on paper and printing them, when neither

71

paper nor print nor electricity nor machines nor newspapers nor magazines will survive the next thirty or forty years. Wouldn't it be best if one were interested in what would survive, wouldn't it be best just if one were to deal only in those forms which are memorizable and singable and which could survive beyond the printing press, if one were interested in "immortality."[35]

However, Ginsberg's commitment to the fulfillment of his vatic role was, fortunately, never abandoned. In fact, to ensure that his themes of death, doom, and eternity would achieve the impact he desired, he invented techniques for writing that would emphasize his message and become, in themselves, an important part of the prophetic mode. An example of one such technique was his desire to write in an "illuminative seizure"—a form of writing which he described as "a yoga that invokes Lord mind."[36]

***

As we have seen, from 1948–63 Ginsberg was preoccupied with the possibility of regaining the sense of "total consciousness" he had experienced during his Blake visions. He had the ambition to recreate that kind of awareness and to write poem-prophecies during an illuminative seizure. In several poems such as "Aether," written under the spell of various drugs, he was able to capture the desired sense of cosmic awe. But, in the late forties and during the fifties, psychedelic drugs were not available; consequently, Ginsberg relied on his studies in consciousness to induce the state of mind, the visionary glow, he wished his readers to share.

From the first, Ginsberg realized that the mind has scores of infinitely brief flashes into the essence of things, so he tried to train his consciousness to be constantly aware of these fleeting glimpses of "high epiphanous mind":[37]

So I try to write during those "naked moments" of epiphany the illumination that comes every day a little bit. Some moment every day, in the bathroom, in bed, in the middle of sex, in the middle of walking down the street, in my head, or not at all. So if it doesn't come at all, then

72

that's the illumination. So then I try and write in that too. So that's like a rabbinical Jewish Hassidic trick that way. So I try to *pay attention all the time*. [38]

He began to think of writing as a high form of meditation, the object of which is to reach into the consciousness and achieve a heightened awareness, a greater attention. The more focused his mind, the more Ginsberg approached the desired illuminative seizure. When he practiced this meditative technique, he would always consider the writing as though it were a sacred art, indicative of the seriousness and holiness of his *vatic* role:

> The writing itself, the sacred act of writing, when you do anything of this nature, is like prayer. The act of writing being done sacramentally, if pursued over a few minutes, becomes like a meditation exercise which brings on a recall of detailed consciousness that is an approximation of high consciousness. High epiphanous mind. So, in other words, writing is a yoga that invokes Lord mind. [39]

By learning to focus on each detail that flashes into the mind, Ginsberg was able to achieve this "approximation of high consciousness." The finer the focus, the deeper the prophetic seizure. His favorite form of meditation was to walk through the streets of New York (one is reminded of Whitman) with a notebook and pencil in hand, focusing on every possible detail:

> So you walk down the city streets in New York for a few blocks, you get this gargantuan feeling of buildings. You walk all day you'll be at the verge of tears. More detail, more attention to the significance of all that robotic detail that impinges on the mind, and you realize through your own body's fears that you are surrounded by a giant robot machine which is crushing and separating people, removing them from nature and removing them from living and dying. But it takes walking around all day to get into that state. [40]

All day Ginsberg would compose using this sacramental method, trying to achieve a "detailed consciousness that is an approximation of high consciousness. High epiphanous mind."[41] The longer he could sustain his meditative concentration, the higher his state of illumination. In fact, many of his great works, like "Howl" and "Kaddish," were written in this manner, with Ginsberg sometimes going on for two days or so, with a generous use of amphetamines to fight off exhaustion.

The single most important aspect of this type of writing is, of course, what the mind focuses on. Obviously, if Ginsberg is walking down the streets of Manhattan in a highly sensitive state of mind, he is going to write poems about the ruthless anonymity of modern civilization; he gets "this gargantuan feeling of buildings"[42] that makes him feel he is "surrounded by a giant robot machine which is crushing and separating people."[43] Therefore, the physical surroundings become a major motif in many of Ginsberg's poems. Not only the actual details of what he is perceiving, but the choice of place determines the theme of the poem. For example, in "Over Kansas" (1954), Ginsberg is writing in an airplane, flying from San Francisco to New York. The poem begins wth epiphanous detail seen "from bus window / on the way to Oakland airport."[44] The overall framework of the poem continues in this manner, from the airport bus, to the "dim brick lounge,"[45] to the airplane itself. During each of these settings, Ginsberg's focus is on himself in relation to what he is seeing. In other words, the physical circumstances of his meditative exercise become the motif of the poem. For example, while he is in the "dim brick lounge," he playfully mocks the businessmen waiting to board the plane, claiming that they are flying away from their troubles. He mocks them with the question "Where shall I fly / not to be sad, my dear?"[46] When he is flying over Hollywood, the meditation turns to the "starry world below" where he sadly announces that all the dreams and fantasies of show business can't affect the "emptiness of the soul." In the airport lounge, the poem details Ginsberg's perceptions of that environment; while he is in the airplane, the poem moves to his insights about Hollywood seen below, and so on. Thus, theme and structure unite in the most simple, direct manner. The prophetic consciousness that he strives to attain during composition results in a poem that is a graph of the mind—in the sense discussed earlier—which is determined by the actual place in which Ginsberg is writing. The art consists in paying attention to the actual movements of the mind, stimulated by the physical surroundings, with a heightened awareness that perceives the very essence of things because the mind is trained in writing as a form of yoga.

The use of physical surroundings, both as theme and structure, first appeared in Ginsberg's poems while he was still writing in his abstract, symbolic style. The poem was "Ode to the Setting Sun" (1949–50). It is a particularly interesting poem not only because it is one of his first attempts at using place as a meditative framework, but because it is a prototype for his most succesful prophetic poem using this technique, "Sunflower Sutra." In "Ode" Ginsberg uses a setting that includes a locomotive and a sunset in order to prompt his meditations on death and transcendence. While watching "The wrathful East of smoke and iron"—the train, heading for the horizon where the sun is setting—Ginsberg muses on the "Dominion of the night / the hosts of prophecy," and concludes that as the day must die, so must man accept "the skull in Eternity." The poem ends with Ginsberg using the landscape and the locomotive as symbols of his own struggle in life, with his "bones carried on the train"[47] into the setting sun (death). There are many other poems in the early period, from 1949–54, that use this meditative and structural technique. In "The Trembling of the Veil" (an imitation of Yeats' work) Ginsberg is looking out of a window, meditating on the wind. In "Cezanne's Ports" he is meditating on Cezanne's painting "L'Estaque" and using the painter's landscape as a point of departure for a discussion of Heaven and Eternity. "Marijuana Notation" has Ginsberg once again looking out of a window and drawing the physical surroundings into a contemplation of Eternity. "Siesta in Xbalba" was partly written while Ginsberg sat at the foot of Mount Don Juan in the midst of Mayan ruins in southern Mexico, where "ancient craftsmen came to complete work left unfinished at their death."[48] Ginsberg journeyed there in 1954, hoping to compose in an illuminative seizure, inspired by the traditional setting of ancient shaman-prophets.

By 1955, when Ginsberg had reached the mature style of "Howl," he had mastered the technique of using his physical surroundings as both a thematic and structural foundation. In "Sunflower Sutra" the motif is so natural that it seems perfectly appropriate for Ginsberg to undergo a transcendental experience while sitting in the shade of a Southern Pacific locomotive, meditating on a sunflower. This same kind of transcendental, prophetic experience is recorded in another poem of this period, "Transcription of Organ Music," in which Ginsberg is contemplating a flower in a peanut bottle, while desperately trying to induce a visionary sensation:

> The flower in the glass peanut bottle formerly
>   in the kitchen crooked to take a place in
>   the light
> the closet door opened, because I used it before,
>   it kindly stayed open waiting for me, its
>   owner.
>
> I began to feel my misery in pallet on floor,
>   listening to music, my misery, that's why I
>   want to sing,
> The room closed down on me, I expected the
>   presence of the Creator...[49]

Here he is masterfully using his physical surroundings to force himself into a visionary state, yearning for the clarity and heightened awareness of his Blake visions. He even admits his prophetic calling, openly declaring that he wants people to bow as they see him and say he is gifted with poetry; he has seen the presence of the Creator. The use of his room, the flower, his pallet, and some unnamed ethereal music in the background all converge in the poem to give it a thematic resolution; that is, Ginsberg manages to convey a sense of creation as his mind travels from object to object in the room. Thus, the poetic line follows the thought.

Other poems were to follow using this same technique, with minor variations. "In the Baggage Room at Greyhound," Ginsberg makes use of the baggage room and the travelers' baggage to represent a symbolic, spiritual journey with passengers "looking for a bus to ride us back home to Eternity."[50] "A Strange New Cottage In Berkeley," "Sather Gate Illumination," "My Sad Self," "Sunset S.S. Azemour," and many others use physical surroundings in an attempt to grasp a transcendental vision, with Ginsberg always trying to be worthy of his *vatic* role by penetrating, in vision, the space around him.

76

This technique has been pervasive throughout his career. As recently as 1975, while on a Buddhist retreat, he wrote several haikus of this sort:

> Cabin in the Rockies
>
> Sitting on a tree stump with half a cup of tea
> sun down behind mountains—
> Nothing to do.

> An hour after dawn
> I haven't thought of Buddha once yet!
> —walking back into the retreat house.[51]

As in his previous use of this technique, the form is determined by his use of the surrounding detail. In the first haiku, Ginsberg sits on a tree stump drinking tea; the next line is another description of the physical surroundings; this is followed by the last line, a seemingly simple thought based on the Buddhist notion of transcendental emptiness!

***

There are other aspects of Ginsberg's poetics that also result from his technique of writing while in a "prophetic illuminative seizure," that would ultimately induce the same or a similar consciousness in his reader. After years of practice, writing in sessions that often took all day, Ginsberg realized that he could compose his poems in rhythmic units that correspond not only to the thought (as discussed in the previous section), but to his actual breathing pattern. After he had written the "Moloch" section of "Howl" (1955), he became intrigued by the possibility of catalyzing his consciousness in his reader by arranging the rhythmic units to correspond exactly with his own breathing at the time of composition:

> ...the rhythmic units that I'd written down were basically breathing exercise forms which if anybody else repeated would catalyze in them the same pranyic breathing physiological spasm that I was going through, and so would presumably catalyze in them the same affects or emotions.[52]

This realization was an extension of the experiments he had

first conducted back in the early fifties when he was arranging his prose journal writings into verse, trying to please William Carlos Williams. However, his concern with breath was then more related to actual talking-breath rhythms, i.e., notating by line arrangement the natural breath patterns of normal speech:

> . . .I went over my prose writings, and I took out little four or five line fragments that were absolutely accurate to somebody's speak-talk-thinking and rearranged them in lines, according to breath, according to how you'd break it up if you were actually to talk it out . . . The influence was that originality of taking materials from your own existence . . . you articulate *your* rhythm, your own rhythms.[53]

His interest in breath and natural breathing units, then, began early. However, it was not fully realized until he had written the "Moloch" section of "Howl," which was composed under the influence of peyote during his exploration of extraordinary states of consciousness:

> I had an apt. on Nob Hill, got high on Peyote, & saw an image of the robot skullface of Moloch in the upper stories of a big hotel glaring into my window . . . I wandered down Powell Street muttering, "Moloch, Moloch" all night & wrote *Howl* II nearly intact in cafeteria at foot of Drake Hotel, deep in the hellish vale.[54]

The "hellish vale" is a combination of peyote and the meditative practice of focusing attention to induce the prophetic illuminative seizure. After writing the "Moloch" section, Ginsberg realized the rhythmic units were based on his breathing (aligned with thought units); he believed that anyone reading Part II (i.e., the "Moloch" section) properly, would have to *breathe* exactly the way he was breathing while in the heightened state of awareness, the "hellish vale." He had unconsciously transcribed his prophetic vision into rhythmic units that corresponded to his "breathing physiological spasm."[55] The amazing thing about this theory-practice is that it actually works. When the reader says the units aloud, in an excited mood, making sure he breathes with each rhythmic break, the experience can actually approach Ginsberg's original breath-mind-feeling patterns. Therefore, by going through the same breathing "spasm" the reader "would presumably catalyze in himself the same *affects* or emotions."[56]

> Moloch the incomprehensible prison! Moloch the
> crossbone soulless jailhouse and Congress
> of sorrows! Moloch whose buildings are
> judgement! Moloch the vast stone of war!
> Moloch the stunned governments![57]

Ginsberg believes that his visionary episodes in Harlem were partly a result of his unconscious syncopation with Blake's breath units while he was reading "The Little Girl Lost," *et al.*, that eventful night:

> So you find in Blake or any good poetry a series of vowels which if you pronounce them in proper sequence *with the breathing* indicated by the punctuation, as in ... "Howl," the Moloch section ... you find a yogic breathing. Yogic's a bad word 'cause it's un-American—you find a "phys.-ed" breathing that, *if reproduced by the reader*, following the poet's commas and exclamation points and following long long long breaths, will get you high physiologically ... will actually deliver a buzz like grass, or higher. And so I think that's what happened to me in a way with Blake.[58]

By following the rhythmic units, as indicated by punctuation (as Ginsberg did in 1948 while reading Blake), the reader can actually experience the "prophetic illuminative seizure" that Ginsberg underwent on peyote and transferred into the "Moloch" section of "Howl." The underlying assumption of this theory is that breath is ultimately the "director" of an individual's emotional pattern, that in pronouncing the words and repeating the breathing patterns the reader will experience the emotion the poet is trying to convey. Putting it in a simple formula, it would be something like this: Ginsberg's rhythmic units are dictated by his breathing patterns; the breathing patterns in turn are controlled by the particular emotion he is experiencing; thus, the emotions give rise to the breath which is notated by rhythmic units separated by punctuation and articulated in words. Language, in this schema, the language of poetry, becomes an extension of the physiology of the body. As Ginsberg puts it:

79

Mainly from this point of view: that the words we pronounce do connect finally to our body, connect to our breathing, particularly, and breathing connects to feeling, feeling articulated in language. Poetry is a rhythmic vocal articulation of feeling and the content of poetry is feeling as well as whatever else you would call it if it were removed from feeling—I suppose conditioned reflex language chain associations.[59]

So he realized, after writing the "Moloch" section, that it was possible for him to give forth prophetic rhapsodies and change consciousness by carefully inducing in his reader the same breathing units he was experiencing during his meditative, illuminative writing periods—"you can teach breathing... inspiration being a matter of breath."[60]

Ginsberg's first great experiment in *consciously* writing inspired poetry, which notates breathing patterns, is to be found in Part II of "Kaddish." Here Ginsberg uses the dash as indication of his breath units, trying to coordinate breath with thought (words) in order accurately to express the illuminative state of mind he was experiencing in the painful recall of his life with his mother Naomi. Once again, to ensure heightened consciousness, Ginsberg used drugs to stimulate his awareness and help him achieve, not only "all day long attention," but on this occasion, almost two days of intense meditative concentration. (He used injections of amphetamine to keep him going, "plus a little bit of morphine, plus some dexedrine later, because it was all in one long sitting."[61]) The use of amphetamines helped him attain the "peculiar metaphysical tinge" he was after in recording his prophecy of death and doom—using, as he had so often, the method of minute particulars to capture the essence of Naomi's life and death:

> ...the language intuitively chosen as in trance & dream, the rhythms rising thru breath from belly to breast, the hymn completed in tears, the movement of the physical poetry demanding and receiving decades of life while chanting Kaddish the names of Death in many mind-worlds the self seeing the Key to life found at last in our own self.[62]

80

"Kaddish" is a "physical poetry" with "the rhythms rising thru breath" becoming feelings, i.e., from the body ("belly") to the "breast" (emotions). As in the "Moloch" section of "Howl," the notation is made to correspond to the emotions by a careful use of punctuation to indicate breathing units:

> Your last night in the darkness of the Bronx—
> I phone-called—thru hospital to secret police.
> That came, when you and I were alone, shrieking
> at Elanor in my ear—who breathed hard in her own
> bed, got thin—
> Now will forget, the doorknock, at your
> fright of spies,—Law advancing, on my honor—
> Eternity entering the room—you running to the
> bathroom undressed, hiding in protest from the
> last heroic fate—
> staring at my eyes, betrayed—the final cops
> of madness rescuing me—from your foot against
> the broken heart of Elanor . . .[63]

The dashes indicate Ginsberg's breath while he was composing. If the reader reads the poem with this in mind, the theory is that he will experience the same, or similar, "metaphysical tinge" that Ginsberg underwent while writing about and remembering his mother. The *Word*, language, actually becomes a spiritual alchemy, where the reader is catalyzed, by the manipulation of breathing units in the poem, to experience "the same *affects* or emotions."[64]

Ginsberg would experiment with this method of writing throughout the sixties, refining the accuracy of notation with the use of an Uher tape recorder (which was given to him by Bob Dylan). He realized that he could be true to his breath and thought by dictating the poem and transcribing it later, carefully indicating (by punctuation or line arrangement) the breath and thought units as they were accurately recorded on tape. He could tell where the thought and breath broke because the Uher made a clicking sound every time he turned it off, which meant he had completed one thought-breath and was beginning another. So, his dedication to his theory during these experiments with the tape recorder resulted in an absolute accuracy, to the point of being able to record the mind in its natural rate of flow (impossible if he were writing in longhand, or using a typewriter, because both methods would impose their own rhythms, due to the time factor, or—in the case of the typewriter—the rhythms of the machine would impinge on the rhythms of natural thought and breath[65]). An example of his use of coordinating rhythmic units with the aid of the Uher recorder is the poem "Wichita Vortex Sutra" (1966), which was written in a series of very long meditative sittings while he was traveling through Kansas—dictating his poem as he went:

That the rest of earth is unseen,
an outer universe invisible,
Unknown except thru
language
airprint
magic images
or prophecy of the secret
heart the same
in Waterville as Saigon one human form . . .[66]

Listening to the actual recording, it became clear that Ginsberg, instead of using dashes as he did in "Kaddish," notated breath and thought breaks by line arrangement. In other words, when the line breaks, the actual breath and thought breaks. After each break there was a click on the tape, indicting end of thought-breath. The poem actually *sounded* like this:

That the rest of earth is unseen (Click!)
an outer universe invisible (Click!)
Unknown (Click!) except thru
(Click!) language
(Click!) airprint
(Click!) magic images
or prophecy of the secret (Click!)
heart the same (Click!)
in Waterville as Saigon one human form (Click!)

Ginsberg has described the method of transcription he used in this poem as follows:

> So when transcribing, I pay attention to the clicking on and
> off of the machine, which is . . . the equivalent of how they
> arrive in the mind and how they're vocalized on the tape
> recorder.[67]

He finally arrived at a method of composition that didn't
interfere with his attempts accurately to "pronounce aloud the
thoughts that are going through the head."[68] With the tape
recorder, he managed to unite thought and breath in a vivid,
accurate transcription of the mind and the emotions that,
when read as notated, would cause a parallel thought-
emotion-breath in the reader. This was an ideal way for him to
communicate his prophetic consciousness, achieved by long
sessions of meditation and years devoted to consciousness
exploration. He had learned a method of catalyzing emotions
in his readers that might achieve for them the catalyzed
visionary state that Blake had induced in him. After twenty
years, an important technical experiment had yielded a
method of writing in a deep, illuminative seizure, with
minimal interference, from the time of thought-breath-feeling
to actual transcription. The use of his Uher tape recorder
allowed him to pursue "the sacred art of writing"[69] as a
meditation exercise which would "bring on a recall of detailed
consciousness that is an approximation of high consciousness.
High epiphanous mind."[70] The actual method of transcription
facilitated the goal of getting "deeper and deeper into your own
central consciousness"[71] and achieving the transmission of a
prophetic consciousness. This is a method of composition
where "writing is a yoga that invokes Lord mind."[72]

***

Another writing technique that developed from
Ginsberg's daylong meditations was the development of the
catalogue and its various attributes, such as the use of
anaphora, the free association of detail, and a "rhythmic
pulsation" generated as a by-product of the catalogue. Ginsberg
was seeking techniques, during the formative stages of "Howl"
(1954-55), that could meet the requirements of prophetic
versification. By this time, he was consciously working in the

83

prophetic tradition, musing over the difficulties of graphing the movements of the mind. His poetry had to meet the urgent needs of his sense of the "apocalyptic end of history."[73] Later, he would describe the problem as one of discovering

> ...a poetry adequate to that, [the prophetic urgency to communicate a sense of the apocalyptic doom approaching] it's just that we will have taken a realistic estimate of our bodies, of our breath, and of our machinery and our history, and imagined it...[74]

In order to write like this, Ginsberg sought models in literature where the prophetic urge had already been realized.

The first model he found was, naturally, the Bible. He was interested in the long, rambling, free associative catalogues in passages such as these from *The Lamentations of Jeremiah:*

> 2 He hath led me, and brought me into darkness, but not into light.
> 3 Surely against me is he turned; he turneth his hand against me all the day.
> 4 My flesh and my skin hath he made old; he hath broken my bones.
> 5 He hath builded against me, and compassed me with gall and travail.
> 6 He hath set me in dark places, as they that be dead of old.
> 7 He hath hedged me about, that I cannot get out; he hath made my chain heavy.[75]

The obvious characteristic of this passage is the use of the catalogue of Jeremiah's lamentations to underscore his afflictions. God *hath* done this and *hath* done that, and so on. Ginsberg was impressed by this litany of complaint; he realized that it was a form that allowed a kind of free association of thought. The catalogue, in Ginsberg's interpretation, allowed the writer to link together the mind's thoughts in a natural way without any restraints of linear structure or logical connection. It seemed a perfect way for him to record the explorations in consciousness he performed in his daily writing-meditation sessions, a way for him to be true to the mind without any encroachment of pre-determined form or literary decorum.

84

His literary model for the catalogue in writing "Howl" was not, perhaps surprisingly, Whitman, but the 18th century poet Christopher Smart in his catalogues: *Jubilate Agno* ("Rejoice in the Lamb"). Ginsberg was interested in Smart because he was a visionary lauded by Blake, and had also spent time in a mental institution. When Ginsberg read Smart's *Jubilate*, he was impressed by the use of the catalogue and the contemporary quality of the verse:

> For I will consider my Cat Jeoffrey.
> For he is the servant of the Living God, duly
>   and daily serving him.
> For at the first glance of the glory of God
>   in the East he worships in his way.
> For is this done by wreathing his body seven
>   times round with elegant quickness.
> For then he leaps up to catch the musk, which
>   is the blessing of God upon his prayer.
> For he rolls upon prank to work it in.
> For having done duty and received blessing he
>   began to consider himself.[76]

As in the passage from Jeremiah, the poet isn't concerned with a linear progression or development of an argument or a classical beginning, middle, and end. He is, as Ginsberg noted, merely free-associating. Ginsberg was also impressed with the rhythmic pulsation that the Hebrew prophet and Smart both employed. In Jeremiah, the repetition of "He hath" at the beginning of almost every line created a hypnotic rhythm that was not only indicative of the Hebraic form of prayer, but a technique used in most religious settings to create a feeling of inspiration and piety. Smart used this technique in the repetition of "For" at the beginning of each of his lines. The catalogue, then, presented for Ginsberg not only a model in sound, but a method of free-association that liberated the mind for exploration of epiphanous consciousness. At the same time, by the use of the rhythmic pulsation, this repetitive technique caused a religious feeling approaching that of prayer. So, he began experimenting with the catalogue and its primary techniques in an attempt to write a "beautiful enough prophecy with such exquisite penetrant prosody that the

85

hardest hat will vibrate with delight."[77]

Actually, Ginsberg's first published use of the catalogue (its only use until "Howl") appeared in the poem that is a prototype for "Howl"—"Paterson." Ginsberg uses the catalogue in his condemnation of a repressive society, as exemplified in the second stanza:

> rather jar my body down the road, crying by
> a diner in the Western sun;
> rather crawl on my naked belly over the tincans
> of Cincinatti:
> rather drag a rotten railroad tie to Golgotha
> in the Rockies;[78]

These lines, though written six years prior to "Howl," were not published until 1960, when "Patterson" appeared in *Kulchur #1*. Like Smart's use of "For" and Jeremiah's use of "He hath," Ginsberg's use of "rather" not only creates the rhythm but gives the poem a cohesive form. As in Jeremiah, the poem is a lamentation of woes endured. It has a somewhat hypnotic quality, like a religious litany.

However, the experiments with the catalogue were not fully realized until sometime in 1954, when Ginsberg began the initial sketches for "Howl." By this time, with Kerouac's encouragement, Ginsberg had become interested in jazz, particularly in the saxophone improvisations of Lester Young. Ginsberg saw that Young made use of a recurrent theme in his long, stoned-out riffs that were free-associational. Each riff started with a repeated cadence. Young composed his saxophone score, Ginsberg thought, in a manner similar to the way Smart and Jeremiah wrote, using a catalogue of associations sustained by the repetition of the same or similar initial sound (or series of notes):

> Lester Young, actually, is what I was thinking about ...
> *Lester Leaps in, Howl* is all *Lester Leaps In.* And I got that
> from Kerouac. Or paid attention to it on account of
> Kerouac, surely—he made me listen to it.[79]

Kerouac's insistence that Ginsberg listen to Young and Charlie Parker, among others, resulted in his acceptance of the catalogue as the basic paradigm for "Howl." In his "Notes for Howl and Other Poems," written in 1959, Ginsberg identifies the Hebraic model and the jazz sound as the main inspiration for his experiment in the use of catalogue and the long line. (He added Smart to the list in a 1968 conversation with Mark Robinson, a poet and scholar.) In "Howl Part I," Ginsberg used "who" as his rhythmic base, in the same way Jeremiah used "He hath," Smart used "For," or Lester Young used the same riff to start a catalogue of thematic associations.

Instead of quoting the published version of Part I, it would be more interesting to present an earlier version, with cross-outs and additions, to give the reader a more accurate idea of the original experimentation with catalogue that has become so renowned:

> I saw the best minds of my generation destroyed
> by madness, starving, hysterical, naked, ~~angel-headed hipster~~
> wandering around the negro streets at dawn
> looking for an angry fix, angelheaded hipsters
> looking for the shuddering connection between
> the wheels & wires of the machine of the Night
> who poverty and tatters and ~~fantastic~~ hollow
> eyed and high sat up all night in the supernatural
> darkness of cold water flats floating across
> the tops of cities contemplating jazz,
> who sat in rooms in underwear unshaven
> burning their dollars in wastebaskets listening
> to the Terror through the wall
> who bared their brains to Heaven under the
> El and saw Mohammedan angels staggering on
> tenement roofs illuminated,
> who chained themselves to subways for an endless
> ride from Battery to Holy Bronx until the noise
> of wheels and children brought them down shuddering
> mouth-racked and battered bleak of brain on
> Benzedrine all drained of brilliance in the drear
> light of Zoo,
> who ~~stood~~ sat in the stale bars of xxerning
> afternoon in desolate Euphoric bar listening

to the crack of doom on the hydrogen jukebox,
>who talked continuously seventy hours from
park to pad to bar[80]

This fragment, from a letter to William Burroughs dated "S.F. 1955," was the culmination of Ginsberg's interest in the catalogue, via Jeremiah, Smart, and Lester Young. He was writing a prophecy in the style of Jeremiah's lament, bemoaning the terrible treatment of his "angleheaded hipsters" by a society built on ruthless destruction and doom. He was writing a prophecy in the style of Christopher Smart, using wild flourishes of disconnected images in a collage whose thematic thread is not the cat "Jeoffry," but a catalogue of the terrible events in his friends' lives. He was writing a prophecy in "long, saxophone-like chorus I knew Kerouac would hear the sound of,"[81] which was modeled on the actual saxophone sound of Lester Young, depending on "the word 'who' to keep the beat, a base to keep measure, return to and take off from . . ."[82] In fact, Ginsberg remembers the rhythmic paradigm that was going through his head while he was writing the first sketch of "Howl," quoted above. It was based on one of the cuts off the album, *Lester Leaps In,* and goes something like:

>Dadada DAT DAT DA, dada DA da,
>Dadada DAT DAT DA, dat da DA da,
>Dadada DAT DAT DA, dat da Da da,
>Dadada DAT DAT DA, dat da Da da,
>Dadada
>dadada
>>dada da dadah[83]

The "Dadada" at the beginning of each "line" is analogous to the "who" in "Howl." As in jazz, the idea was to begin a line with the same anaphoric sound and add to it; when finished with the "riff," you return to the "Dadada" or the "who." The *rhythm* of the catalogue, then, becomes the element of control, freeing the mind for associations without the restriction of trying to make sense or follow a linear flow of thought.

This particular use of the catalogue became the basis for several of Ginsberg's poems. Besides using it in the other sections of "Howl," Ginsberg would use the catalogue in this manner in "America," in several parts of "Kaddish," "Lysergic Acid," "Psalm III," "Tears," and many others during the late fifties and early sixties.

Ginsberg's prophetic quest had a significant influence on his poetics, as demonstrated in his use of physical surroundings, the breath notation of his line, and the use of the catalogue. Each of these innovations was a part of his artful devotion to the study of consciousness. His decision to follow Blake's statement that every man was a prophet led him to a practice of writing that involved deep absorption in meditation. The meditation, in turn, focused on many of the elements discussed in this section. His ultimate prophetic ambition was not only to retrieve the heightened awareness he had experienced in his Blake visions, but to learn how to induce higher states of consciousness in his readers. However, as shown in the following section, Ginsberg's quest for extraordinary or mystical states of being were to prove self-defeating. In fact, after re-examining his fifteen years of devotion to his guru, Blake, he came to the point of having to renounce his visionary master. He felt himself too much under Blake's domination. The obligation he had labored under to follow what he conceived as Blake's "instructions" had led to his denying the here and now. He felt he had denied himself the freedom to be just himself.

V

The Change

My energies of the last . . . oh, 1948 to 1963, all completely
washed up. On the train in Kyoto having renounced Blake,
renounced visions, renounced *Blake!* There was a cycle
that began with the Blake visions which ended on the train
in Kyoto when I realized that to attain the depth of
consciousness that I was seeking when I was talking about
the Blake vision, that in order to attain it I had to cut
myself off from the Blake vision and renounce it. Otherwise I'd be hung up on a memory of an experience. Which
is not the actual awareness of now, now. In order to get
back to now, in order to get back to the total awareness of
now and contact with what was going on around me, or
direct vision of the moment, now I'd have to give up this
continual churning thought process of yearning back to a
visionary state.

—*Ginsberg, 1965* [1]

***

So given that complication I found it useful after visiting
India to try and simplify my mind a little bit—rather than
intellectually casting around through the window to see if
it was the Eternal Field, maybe try and eliminate all that

90

thought about eternity and concentrate all of my energy
and my effort in one single place . . . something that would
be physiological, involving my body, not just my mind—
that's what yoga is, yoking of the body to the search, the
path that you're into.

—*Ginsberg, April 7, 1971* [2]

***

. . . meeting a lot of holy men in India. Yeah, that changed
me. You see, mainly getting over the fear of an absolute god
outside of myself and coming to a slow realization that the
divinity which was prophesied to me by Blake years ago
was actually in myself rather than outside like a hidden
god outside the universe . . . the change for me finally was a
precipitation of my awareness back into my body from
wandering in various alternative possible metaphysical
universes experienced in visions or experienced under
drugs.

—*Ginsberg, October 1964* [3]

Even at the very beginning of his quest in 1948, after his
Blake visions, Ginsberg began to feel a sense of inadequacy
because of the vows he had made. The attempt to annihilate
consciousness, his role as poet-prophet, the confrontations
with death and doom, the striving for cosmic consciousness,
all overwhelmed him to such an extent that there were times
he doubted his ability to continue. In particular, the horrible
fears of the "cosmic demonic" vision of death—"my death and
also the death of being itself"[4]—appeared as such a threat that,
at first, he wanted to forget the whole thing. He thought that
his quest might not even be human because the

. . . consciousness itself was so vast, much more vast than
any idea of it I'd had or any experience I'd had, that it was
not even human anymore—and was in a sense a threat,
because I was going to die into that inhuman ultimately. [5]

At that time, he says he felt too cowardly to undertake the task.
In fact, this uneasiness never entirely left him throughout all

the years of his quest.

Yet, Ginsberg had vowed never to deny or forget the oath he had made to explore consciousness in search of the cosmic awareness to which he had been exposed. Consequently, Ginsberg pursued, though reluctantly at times, his experiments, trying to reach beyond his human frailty and his fears of the serpent monsters of death. He would learn in his studies how to achieve extraordinary meditative-writing states in which his experiments yielded insights into civilization's doom and his own death, as well as discoveries of his own poetic practice. In "Aether," and in the several drug poems at the end of *Kaddish and Other Poems* written under the influence of the Amazon psychedelic Ayahuasca, Ginsberg was able to experience "different levels and different similarities and different reverberations of the same vision."[6] In "Aether" he stands on a balcony waiting for a total change of consciousness; in the Ayahuasca poem he encounters the "faceless Destroyer"—death. But, the whole Blakean quest, culminating in his drug experiments of the late fifties and early sixties, became such a burden that Ginsberg felt he was "painting" himself into a corner:

> ...that corner being an inhuman corner in the sense that I figured I was expanding my consciousness, and I had to go through with it, but at the same time I was confronting this serpent monster, so I was getting in a real terrible situation. It finally would get so if I'd take the drugs I'd start vomiting. But I felt that I was duly bound and obliged for the sake of consciousness expansion, and insight, and breaking down my identity...[7]

By 1961, Ginsberg's dedication to the poetics of vision and the Gates of Wrath was itself becoming an obstacle to further awareness. He began wondering whether he was actually moving in the right direction, because his constant "yearning back" to Blake was only inducing in him a sense of the inhuman and otherworldly, instead of a clear perception of the space around him—what Charles Olson calls "The Human Universe." Besides, the drug visions were becoming so horrendous that he would start vomiting because of the monstrous images of death that he was constantly conjuring up.

Therefore, toward the end of 1961, in search of guidance, Ginsberg made a spiritual pilgrimage to India. On his way to India he stopped in Israel to consult the philosopher Martin Buber. Ginsberg's friend, Peter Orlovsky, accompanied him:

> We called him up and made a date and had a long conversation ... Peter asked him what kind of visions he'd had in bed when he was younger. But he said he was *not* any longer interested in visions like that. The kind of visions he came up with were more like spiritualistic table rappings ... rather than big beautiful seraphic Blake angels.[8]

Ginsberg told Buber that he was beginning to think of his study of consciousness as headed in the wrong direction. In his drug quests and during his long, meditative sittings, he was experiencing loss of identity and confronting the non-human world. He explained that he had believed it his responsibility to evolve and change completely and perhaps also to become non-human; Buber advised Ginsberg to become more interested in human relationships, that the important thing was to accept living in a human universe and not get caught up in the "human and the non-human."[9] Ginsberg appreciated Buber's advice, for he had already begun to think along this line himself.

When Ginsberg and Orlovsky got to India, they visited as many holy men as they could, always telling them about the Blake visions and about the resulting predicament Ginsberg was faced with at this point along the spiritual path. In Rishikesh, Swami Shivananda told him "Your own heart is your guru."[10] This formula made a deep impression on Ginsberg. The swami told him to devote more attention to his emotions, rather than to conjuring up imaginary universes in his mind. By directing Ginsberg to his heart, he meant that Ginsberg should stop trying to transcend the body and, instead, give more energy to "inhabiting the human form."[11] In other words, the psychic problem that Ginsberg was beginning to work out was that

93

...for various reasons it had seemed to me at one time or another that the best thing to do was to drop dead. Or not be afraid of death but go into death. Go into the non-human, go into the cosmic so to speak; that God was death, and if I wanted to attain God I had to die. So I thought that what I was put up to was to therefore break out of my body, if I wanted to attain complete consciousness.[12]

But Shivananda told him to stop avoiding the body, i.e., life now in the human form, to stop trying to attain an other worldly consciousness by constructing imaginary universes.

After several other gurus had told Ginsberg the same thing, he began to re-examine his Blake experience once again, from this new perspective. He wondered if Blake's instructions had really been to annihilate ordinary consciousness. Perhaps the message was more that he should accept "The Human Form Divine," and that Blake had meant Ginsberg to accept his certain death and stop trying to get beyond it. All the holy men Ginsberg met told him that he was divine right now, that he didn't have to seek divinity. The problem, according to Ginsberg, was

...mainly getting over the fear of an absolute god outside of myself and coming to a slow realization that the divinity which was prophesied to me by Blake years ago was actually in myself rather than outside like a hidden god outside the universe... the change for me finally was a precipitation of my awareness back into my body from wandering in various alternative possible metaphysical universes experienced in visions or experienced under drugs.[13]

While Ginsberg was traveling through India, then, he was tremendously preoccupied with the problem of the acceptance of the body. He was reconsidering his attempts to reach past death and into the non-human. He realized that the divinity prophesied to him by Blake was to be sought inside him and not as the object of a quest for cosmic consciousness. Yet, the advice of the Indian holy men and that of Martin Buber was also very interesting—he was faced with the realization that the

94

last fifteen years of his life had been the result of a misdirection. When he visited the exile camp of the Tibetan refugees and talked to the Lama Dujom Rinpoche, he was further alarmed when the holy man told him not to cling to any experiences, whether they be human or non-human. Ginsberg had been clinging to his Blake visions ever since that night in Harlem; indeed, he had built the major part of his poetics on his visionary quest. But, by always harking back to Harlem, he actually was cutting himself off from "direct perception whether it was visionary or ordinary."[14] The Tibetan Lama's advice convinced him that he had to let go, to stop clinging to Blake. The exact instructions of Dujom Rinpoche were:

> If you see anything beautiful, don't cling to it. If you see anything horrible, don't cling to it.[15]

Therefore, by the time he left India and had spent a few weeks in Japan sitting with Gary Snyder in formal Zen style, contemplating the meaning of his recent spiritual pilgrimage and the unavoidable similarity of the different gurus' advice, he was on the verge of renouncing his visionary quest altogether. The actual breaking point came while he was on a train from Kyoto to Tokyo, en route to the Vancouver Poetry Festival:

> ...where all of a sudden I renounce drugs, I don't renounce drugs but I suddenly didn't want to be dominated by the non-human any more, or even be dominated by the moral obligation to enlarge my consciousness any more. Or do anything except *be* my heart—which just desired to be and be alive now.[16]

It was while riding on the train that Ginsberg, in his words, "renounced visions—renounced *Blake*—too."[17] His renunciation marked the end of a cycle that had begun

> ...with the Blake vision and which ended on the train in Kyoto when I realized that to attain the depth of consciousness that I was seeking when I was talking about the Blake vision, that in order to attain it I had to cut myself off from the Blake vision and renounce it.[18]

Ginsberg had rid himself of a burden and was now free to accept himself in his own form as he was. He felt that his quest

95

was ending, that he no longer had to attain a supernatural vision. Instead, there was nothing more to fulfill, except beyond the human. The relief was so great that he started weeping on the train. And in the midst of his emotion, true to form, realizing that the moment was a kind of illuminative seizure, he pulled out his pencil and started recording the breakthrough that he had achieved:

> Fortunately I was able to write then, too: "So that I do live I will die"—rather than be cosmic consciousness, immortality, Ancient of Days, perpetual consciousness existing forever.[19]

The line he is quoting in the above passage is from the poem-record of this breakthrough experience, "The Change: Kyoto-Tokyo Express":

> In my train seat I renounce
> my power, so that I do
> live I will die . . .[20]

"The Change" (written July 18, 1963) is Ginsberg's attempt at mystical exorcism. It is a head-on confrontation with the fears of cosmic doom and an announcement that he is abandoning his vows to Blake. He wanted to continue his studies, but without the burden of always striving "to get beyond," to attain the cosmic. He was still interested in this, but not in the sense that he had been pursuing it under the supernatural guidance of Blake. The method of his exorcism paralleled the Tibetan Buddhist meditation technique that Ginsberg learned from Dujom Rinpoche. It is called the *Sattipathana* Meditation, a series of techniques aimed at the complete exploration of bodily fears of death and at trying to get the practitioner to be grounded—i.e., to stop desiring transcendence, to stop conjuring up ideas of a blissful other world, to accept the human form and its natural process of decay. The technique is explained by the British psychologist David Cooper, also a student of a Tibetan Lama, as

> . . . the deep exploration of fantasies of killing oneself in different ways, the free-flowing experience of images of mutilated corpses, forms of torture, bodily putrefaction after death . . .[21]

Cooper's explanation is a good gloss on Ginsberg's Sattipathana of death in "The Change," where he is desperately trying to accept his mortal body, and so exorcise the dreaded "dragon of Death" that had possessed him ever since his Harlem visions:

> Let the dragon of Death
> come forth from his
> picture in the whirling
> white clouds' darkness
>
> And suck dream brains &
> claim these lambs for his
> meat, and let him feed
> and be other than I
>
> Till my turn comes I
> enter the maw and change
> to a blind rock covered
> with misty ferns that
> I am not all now . . .[22]

Here is the *Sattipathana* technique of exploring death through images of it. There is no annihilation of consciousness, no reaching beyond death, but acceptance of the body. Finally, he declares that he is just an ordinary human being, not a "dragon or / God":

> but a universe of skin and breath
> & changing thought and
> burning hand & softened
> heart in the old bed of
> my skin . . .[23]

Earlier in the poem he speaks of himself as "that worm soul . . . trembling to die,"[24] an allusion to the worm of death in Blake's "The Sick Rose." However, with the *Sattipathana* and with his accepting the advice of the Indian holy men, he was now able to claim that he had finally "come sweetly / now back to my Self as I was."[25] Over and over he announced that he has come back to his human form, completely accepting himself as he is—"I am that I am."[26]

When Ginsberg got back to North America and was attending the Vancouver Poetry Conference, the validity of his new experience was reinforced by many of the other poets there. He heard Charles Olson saying "I am one with my skin,"[27] and Ginsberg linked this with what Creeley had been long insisting on. Creeley's terminology for the acceptance of the body and the rejection of non-human, cosmic awareness, was "the place," or, in Ginsberg's words:

> ...the place we are. Meaning this place, here. And trying to like, be real in the real place to be aware of the place where he is.[28]

Creeley and Olson were demanding that the poet be who he is where he is, and that made a great impression on Ginsberg, since he had just reached a similar position. He had completed his metaphysical wanderings, and the task in the remaining years of the 1960's and during the seventies would be to learn how to grow more and more into his body and become part of the here and now, at one with his own skin. The change, then, was

> ...a precipitation of my awareness back into my body from wandering in various alternative possible metaphysical universes experienced in visions...[29]

His discipleship with Blake had ended; in the future he would turn more and more to the East for guidance, including an apprenticeship to the study of mantras through long sessions of chanting. In 1971, he would become a disciple of the Tibetan Lama, Chögyam Trungpa, a colleague of Dujom Rinpoche, and learn how to "ground" himself by means of various Mahayana Tibetan Buddhist meditation techniques. The poetics of vision, 1948–63, had accounted for several successful experiments in consciousness and for the techniques that had produced "Howl" and "Kaddish". He wouldn't abandon those discoveries, nor renounce the poems, but his thematic quests would know a strong shift. The shift would be towards themes of sexuality, towards mantra-poetry, and towards Buddhist *Dharma* messages of self-acceptance and "groundedness."[30] The Change that he had begun to experience throughout India, that culminated on the train to Tokyo and was reinforced in Vancouver, indicated that this cycle of the study of consciousness was completed. His new studies would be founded on explorations in the reality of the self, on self-desire and the desires of others, and on acceptance of his human form in the real world. When, in 1964, he finally returned to New York and agreed to an interview on the subject of his change, Ginsberg postulated some of his new preoccupations:

> You know what I would like—what Paradise I would like to see now? My vision of earthly paradise at this point, if I'm going to come back to my body and accept earth (the place!)—and accept my body and accept and be willing to die—*That*, that acceptance is my desire of life, my paradise . . . the problem now is how do you identify the self once you've got back to the self? Is it really your self? What is your heart? Is it desire? The desire-thing and heart and feeling are infinite. So the question is the realization of what is our real desire and what does everybody really desire?[31]

VI

Post Script: The Visionary Company

Paul Portugés: *Allen, had you been reading a lot of mystical literature prior to your Blake visions?*

Allen Ginsberg: Yeah, I was going to say St. John of the Cross, a little of Plato's *Phaedrus*, and some Plotinus. I had a lot of theology literature at hand from a student from whom I'd sublet an apartment. And St. Teresa of Avila, Blake.[1]

***

It spoke aloud from its Center
one human voice that sounded like an eye—
that made the world visible in my 21st year
and all twenty years before a dream-life
       just waiting for this Blink
         of Consciousness
known by St. John of the Cross . . .

       —*Ginsberg, 1961, from an*
        unpublished manuscript[2]

Ginsberg's propensity for vision was not entirely a matter

of chance. He didn't find himself alone in his Harlem apartment one late afternoon, experiencing those extraordinary visions, without some kind of spiritual preparation. In fact, Ginsberg had been "preparing" himself by studying the visionary literature of Blake, St. John of the Cross, Plotinus, and various accounts of personal, Christian illumination, such as the writings of St. Teresa. He had also been copiously studying the different accounts of vision in William James' *The Varieties of Religious Experience.* In addition, he was particularly impressed by Socrates' comments on poets as "God-intoxicated visionaries" whose only saving grace, he argued with Phaedrus, was their visionary madness. Ginsberg had just read Dostoyevsky's account of a young visionary in *Raw Youth;* later, he concluded that it was "about a kid who had a vision just like me."[3]

Furthermore, during the period of his visionary experiences, Ginsberg even consulted, from time to time, the collection of mystical literature that had been left in his sublet apartment for him to study:

> Because I was in a very exalted state of mind and the consciousness was still with me—I remember I immediately rushed to Plato and read some great image in the *Phaedrus* about horses flying through the sky, and rushed over to St. John and started reading fragments of *con un no saber sabiendo . . . que me quede balbuciendo,* and rushed to the other part of the bookshelf and picked up Plotinus about the Alone . . .[4]

Ginsberg also alludes to his part in the visionary tradition in an autobiographical stanza of "Howl":

> who studied Plotinus Poe St. John of the Cross
> telepathy and bop kaballa because the
> cosmos instinctively vibrated at their
> feet in Kansas . . .[5]

The most obvious influence, of course, was William Blake. Ginsberg had studied, in particular, the visionary masterpiece, *The Marriage of Heaven and Hell.* In one of the sections of Blake's prose poem, the Biblical prophets Isaiah and Ezekiel are

101

dining with Blake. Within the framework of a vision, they are actually discussing visions:

> The prophets Isaiah and Ezekial dined with me and I asked them how they dared so roundly to assert that God spoke to them; and whether they did not think at the time that they would be misunderstood, & so be the cause of imposition.[6]

Isaiah answers Blake, giving him a clarification of the mystical experience in his reply:

> I saw no God, nor heard any, in a finite organical perception; but my senses discover'd the infinite in everything, and as I was then perswaded, & remain confirm'd, that the voice of honest indignation is the voice of God, I cared not for consequences, but wrote.[7]

Isaiah's answer is particularly interesting because it parallels Ginsberg's own description of the Creator/God and his experience of the infinite. Like Isaiah, he believed he was in the presence of the Divine, that he had heard a "God with a human voice"[8] (though probably not in "a finite organical" sense), and his senses also "discovered the infinite in everything." (Ginsberg's own description is a paraphrase of Isaiah: " . . .I saw into the depths of the universe."[9])

When questioned about the extent of the influence Blake had had on him in this context, Ginsberg replied that it was difficult to assess, particularly in terms of pointing to specific passages and determining the parallels.[10] The important point, he suggested, was not in a one-to-one correspondence, but in the realization that he and Blake were both working in an established visionary tradition. Like his master, he was conscious of some of the qualities necessary for mystical illumination, such as auditory apparitions, sensing a preternatural light, a sensation of the infinite, etc. He also said that he knew Blake wrote poetry while in a visionary trance, and his own ambition was to write as Blake had done. However, Ginsberg's visions were initiated by deep depressions, loneliness, and a sense of frustration, instead of the joyous overflowing trance-like state that Blake had known. Ginsberg confessed that he

102

felt closer, in this respect, to St. Teresa, who like himself, had to suffer grave, psychic distress before experiencing her great visions of Christ.

Ginsberg knew that Blake had been a dealer in Gnostic texts. He has speculated that his prophetic mentor must have dabbled in the opaque, automatic writings of the so-called father of mysticism, Plotinus. Ginsberg, too, had been a student of Plotinus ever since Burroughs gave him a copy of *The Enneads*. There, Plotinus outlines several necessary characteristics of visions, and this made an impact on Ginsberg. Plotinus stresses the importance of an auditory awakening, the feeling of seeing the quotidian world in a new, utterly changed way, and the strange sense of the visionary being infused with a mystical light. Ginsberg was particularly interested in the vision of light that Plotinus outlined, having previously read several accounts of the same phenomenon in James' *The Varieties of Religious Experience*. Plotinus describes the light as independent of the visual faculties:

> . . . the eye is not wholly dependent upon an outside and alien light; there is an earlier light within itself, a more brilliant, which it sees sometimes in a momentary flash . . . this is sight without the act, but it is the truest seeing.[11]

This closely describes Ginsberg's sensations during his first vision, when he says his body "felt light" and a sense of understanding, awe, and wonder possessed him. The visionary light is an experience shared by most mystics. As Mircea Eliade points out, "anyone receiving such an experience undergoes a change of being,"[12] and most mystics have claimed that their vision of light and cosmic understanding definitely changed their entire sense of self. Ginsberg is no exception to the tradition.

The major influence on Ginsberg in relation to his visions came from his reading and re-reading of St. John of the Cross. St. John outlines in a precise and straightforward manner many of the necessary preparations for the visionary path. His major emphasis is on what he terms "The Necessity of Suffering":

103

> So great are the trials, and so profound the darkness, spiritual as well as corporal, through which souls must pass, if they will attain perfection, and no human being can explain them, nor experience describe them. He only who has passed through them, but even he cannot explain them.[13]

Ginsberg felt in complete sympathy with St. John's description of the spiritual aspirant experiencing great trials, a profound darkness, and immense suffering. If these were the initial steps towards spiritual awakening, then Ginsberg knew he was on his way. His breaking with Cassady, the incarceration of his mother, his intense loneliness, friends in jail, and a sense of not knowing what to do with himself once he graduated—all these events in his recent life created his desperate sense of hopelessness and frustration. He had given up, much in the same way that St. John deems necessary for a mystical awakening. Ginsberg actually characterized his sad state in terms of St. John's description of the necessity of suffering:

> Allen Ginsberg: I didn't understand what caused the opening of consciousness [i.e., the Blake visions], except in solitude and inattention and giving up. In other words, I'd given up on love—
>
> Q: *Like out of frustration?*
>
> Allen Ginsberg: No, given up in the sense that St. John of the Cross says that when finally after seeking and seeking you give up, you go into a night of despair, a dark night of the soul . . .[14]

Ginsberg stressed the passive quality of mind that results from so much suffering. Immediately prior to his first vision, he had lapsed into a passionless state "when the soul then is passive, when it's not straining, striving, not seeking . . ."[15] This self-characterization reads like a gloss on St. John's description of the passive state necessary for vision, when the aspirant must become "hollow within."[16]

St. John also suggests meditation, fasting, and solitude to create the right frame of mind, the "psychic equilibrium" necessary to receive mystical revelation. Ginsberg's way of life, living alone for weeks in his apartment, eating only some vegetables, and dabbling in some meditation techniques he had learned from Burroughs, seemed to meet all these requirements. Furthermore, having just masturbated before he heard Blake's voice in the room, Ginsberg was in a profoundly inattentive state of mind, a temporary limbo that he felt immediately upon ejaculation:

> So anyway—there I was in my bed in Harlem . . . jacking off. With my pants open, lying around on the bed by the windowsill, looking out . . . [to] the sky above. And I had just come . . . I had been jacking off while reading . . . There's a kind of interesting thing about, you know, distracting your attention while you jack off . . .[17]

The "interesting thing" Ginsberg is talking about is the state when "the attention is completely open like a blossom."[18] It was at that very moment the visions began, when his entire consciousness was in a state of complete relaxation.

As absurd as the parallel may seem, it is precisely Ginsberg's relaxed mind that St. John would claim as the last preparation before the visionary consciousness opens. Evelyn Underhill, in her monumental study, *Mysticism*, notes in the chapter "Voices and Visions" that a mystic usually hears voices or experiences the cosmic light "when the mind is in a state of deep absorption, without conscious thought."[19] She is paraphrasing St. John who claims visions can only occur "when the mind is collected and reserved."[20]

Ginsberg had also been preparing himself by study in the Jewish mystics, particularly from the Kaballa. In addition, he had been reading a lot of Thomas Vaughan, "the spiritual alchemist,"[21] and the mystical poet Henry Vaughan. Having some brief glimpse of his background in the tradition, it is not altogether surprising that suddenly—at the age of twenty-two, alone in a shabby tenement apartment—Ginsberg should have undergone several classical visionary apparitions. In his own way, he had been preparing himself for several months. His study in Plotinus, his discipleship to Blake, the sad dilemma with Cassady, his separation from his friends, and the absorption of the mystical doctine of St. John of the Cross, were all preparation for the single most important set of events in his career as a poet: the visions of doom and his sense of a cosmic consciousness.

Part II

The Visionary Poetics, 1945–1976:
Conversations with Ginsberg on
Drugs, Mantras, and Tibetan Buddhism

VII

On Drugs

Paul Portugés (P.P.): *When did you first start smoking marijuana?*

Allen Ginsberg (A.G.): In 1945 or '46, when I was in New Orleans. When I got back to New York, I scored some pot on 112th St., near First Avenue, which was a Puerto Rican section. One of my shipmates lived there, the one who first turned me on in New Orleans. I scored about $15 or $20 worth, and then I went up to Columbia to share it with my friends. There wasn't much grass around at that time—even Kerouac and Burroughs had a hard time finding some. I wasn't running in marijuana circles then. And though Bill [William Burroughs, author of *Junkie, Naked Lunch*, etc.—P.P.] had tried drugs, had tried weed before, he wasn't able to score around that period in New York. There hadn't been any around. There'd only been benzedrine inhalers.

P.P.: *Did Burroughs suggest that you start writing with the aid of marijuana?*

A.G.: No, it arose naturally out of smoking. I'd been doing a lot of writing in 1945 on benzedrine, like my series of poems called "Denver Doldrums." Those were written after ingesting benzedrine inhalers. I remember doing a lot of composition while high on benzedrine during that period. But I ran into problems during composition; halfway through, I would get tangled up on a line, trying to revise it. But I ended up building a giant salivaesque spider web of lines that I couldn't decipher later on—fragments, modifications, reconsiderations and scratchings over words with a ball point pen. I finally wrote one long, rhapsodic piece in 1946 on amphetamines, but I couldn't edit it, couldn't ever complete it. So, I finally had to give up trying to write with amphetamines.

P.P.: *Until you wrote "Kaddish"?*

A.G.: Yeah, that was written with the aid of meta-amphetamines—methadrine. But, talking about the 1940's and the inhalers—I did manage to get into a regular cycle of writing with benzedrine. Later, I realized that the poems were just like little chicken scratches all over the paper—constantly revising, sort of like circular feedback, brain waves, spaced out. Too spaced out to be workable. The reason I say all this is that when I turned on to grass, it would have been natural for me to try writing on grass—but, oddly enough, I did very little. But my writing habits were already regular, fixed by then—you know, keeping a notebook and writing any time, any place.

P.P.: *In the late 1940's, you wrote a poem called "Marijuana Notation" [included in* Empty Mirror]. *Was that one of the first grass poems?*

A.G.: Yes, I think that's probably among the first that's directly marijuana. I'm so pleased to have gotten something from grass during that time. Some of the other poems in *Empty Mirror*—like "Psalm 1," and "A Ghost May Come"—were probably written with grass. They have that grass-like clarity and silence and stillness.

P.P.: *How would you characterize the grass high, in terms of its effect on your poetry?*

A.G.: The "Marijuana Notation" poem goes from the general, abstract space-out thought to sudden focus on particular detail. Marijuana tends to amplify the volume of thought in the sense

110

of like voices in your head. They become exaggerated, amplified. That makes you a little more mindful, more sensitive to shifts of attention, to shifts of consciousness in the sense of awe of being in that space. Grass also gives you a little confusion, in terms of time. In fact, you get sort of in love with the radiance of the vast space that you're in, and all the rays of light, and our being, perceptions and sounds. It seems such a long time that you might forget what you heard two minutes ago. So, grass aids in recognizing changes of the mind.

P.P.: *I remember you once saying that your use of grass and other drugs was part of a larger scheme to recall the visionary experience you had in 1948, when you heard William Blake singing across the centuries, beyond the grave... You were talking about breaking down everyday consciousness with the aid of drugs, in order to achieve a higher, or, at least, different mode of consciousness.*

A.G.: The phrase I used then was a "break in consciousness," or a "break in the natural mode of consciousness, the habitual mode."

P.P.: *I think Carlos Castaneda, in his drug quest, calls it "stopping the world."*

A.G.: But I didn't stop the world. My intention was to *catalyze* the world, to catalyze my perceptions so that I would see trees—like in my poem "The Trembling of the Veil" [in *Empty Mirror*]—"as live organisms on the moon!" Live organisms on the moon seems to be otherworldly, as well as humorous.

P.P.: *Did smoking grass ever help you achieve that kind of catalyzed perception?*

A.G.: No, I don't think I ever reached those proportions. There was one time, though, that I remember. It was 1965, at a party in Chelsea, London, with Mick Jagger and an interior decorator friend and some other acquaintances. Somebody gave out some hashish—majun chocolate brownies—that I took with a girlfriend of mine. I remember the eternality of the room swinging and a sense of vertigo. But my girlfriend got hysterical, frightened. She had never smoked grass, and eating the

111

brownies was a mistake. I had to take her home in a taxi. Outside, I saw the moon and was struck by the experience of being able to perceive a totally different London—perhaps in the way William Blake saw it. And then I said to myself, "Am I trying to conjure this up, or has it arrived on its own?" But I realized that it had occurred on its own. The feeling was almost identical to that sense of spaciousness and eternality that I had experienced years earlier with my visions of William Blake. I was experiencing a London that I had never seen before, like finding myself in a Blake poem which goes something like

> This cabinet is formed of gold and
> pearl and crystal shining bright
> And within it opens into a world
> And a little lovely moony night
>
> Another London and its towers . . .

I was having visions of a serene moony crystal cabinet in London, seeing through the imagination in eternity. I tried to point that out to my friend, that the moon was out, that it was very calm and spacious, that it was a lovely, visionary blue London night in a taxicab. I tried to explain to her that we had just turned on with the Queen of England or Princess Margaret or somebody. That it was London aristocracy getting high, and that it seemed like a world shaking event with the power of nature lifting us all to a perception of another London, another Thames.

P.P.: *Was that the only time you had a semi-visionary experience with grass or hashish?*

A.G.: Another time in Tangiers in the sixties on majun with Bill [William Burroughs] . . . but generally there was a period when marijuana would make me tremble a great deal, which I find other people have mentioned too. Trembling with fear and awe.

P.P.: *I feel that uneasiness from time to time when I'm high.*

A.G.: Yeah. It's like original sin, sin in the big universe of Jehovah, or sin in the sense of breaking *dharmic* law, or sin in the sense of clinging—of being trapped in existence, the

112

suffering of existence. Grass sometimes gives you the feeling of your body being mortal, the body dying and the body being fragile...

P.P.: *When I smoke grass, I sometimes become extremely anxious, self-conscious of my breathing, uneasy...*

A.G.: I went through that with marijuana. I was so anxious for a while that I stopped smoking altogether. That was in 1950, '51, '52, '53.

P.P.: *Do you think a lot of the anxiety is due to paranoia?*

A.G.: Yeah, paranoia, *legal paranoia*! The legal paranoia was something that made me tremble occasionally. The trouble was really a fear of getting busted—you know, the police banging down the door.

P.P.: *Maybe the recent trend in decriminalizing will help that fear somewhat. But you were always on the fringe of the drug culture, if not at the center of it. Didn't you start taking morphine before you smoked pot?*

A.G.: Yeah, though I never had a habit. I just sort of messed around here and there. I took it with Burroughs the first time, around the first time that he turned on himself. The morphine high is more or less like a warm bath, a warm relaxing bath. There is a slight pressure in the back of the skull. When injected into the vein, there is a slight tingling sensation throughout the body. There is also a slight nausea in your stomach. You might throw up if you're walking around too much or overloaded with food. There is a sense of peacefulness and meditative calm. Also, there is a sense of centering power, a feeling that everything seems mellow, that pain is gone, and therefore, death couldn't be so bad—maybe. Morphine eases pain. It's the opposite of the trembling on grass, the opposite of the anxiety of grass. It's like calming the whole anxiety, helping you slow down to a painless, material world.

P.P.: *Did you experiment in the late forties and fifties with morphine?*

A.G.: Oh yeah, I was taking morphine every couple of weeks in order to experiment with my writing. In Paris, 1958, I was on

113

heroin a great deal writing such poems as "Death to Van Gogh's Ear," and maybe "At Apollinaire's Grave." I used morphine a lot for writing, I would say—as much as anything, morphine and heroin. Also, I used codeine at one time or another.

P.P.: *Does using drugs such as morphine have to do with some kind of writing problems, like getting started, or like trying to get beyond the boring, uninspired everyday reality?*

A.G.: I think it's more a resistance to writing. I always have this guilt that I'm not prolific at all, that I have to keep writing. So, I always carry notebooks around. But, if I get high, I could sit at my desk and write long poems on separate pieces of paper. Even parts of "Kaddish" were written that way, particularly the first sketches, the lyrical sections written in Paris, "O mother what have I forgotten, O mother what have I left out . . ." and that kind of thing. The actual manuscript for "Kaddish" is in the library at New York University. It was originally sold for a benefit for the Living Theater. When I prepared the manuscript for sale, I put together the different stages of the poem in different envelopes while labeling what drugs they were written on. I think that poem was written mostly on meta-amphetamines, instead of a lot of morphine, particularly the "Narrative" section. The meta-amphetamines helped me through one long sitting, one weekend "Proem" and "Narrative." I think I was able to do the "Proem" section and the "Hymnnn" as well.

P.P.: *Have you ever analyzed your poems in terms of the relationship of content and form to the drug you were using while writing?*

A.G.: All mellow poems seem to emerge out of heroin. Endless meta-political ravings in my journal and other stuff you've seen were written on morphine, on heroin. Yeah, probably all of the political poems in the sixties, all of the journal rhapsodies about politics are related to heroin, like the unpublished "I Hate America." That was probably written on heroin in Paris or New York. You know the poem "On Neal's Ashes"? That's written on morphine, though I'm not sure. Maybe on grass, that's more likely. [Ginsberg reads "On Neal's Ashes."]

114

P.P.: *I really like that, Allen.*

A.G.: Yeah, I like it too. I read this a few months ago during intermission at the Dylan Rolling Thunder concert at Fort Collins, Colorado. I wrote it in the bus coming home from seeing Neal's ashes, a bus coming from Los Gatos to San Francisco. I wrote it in that little pocket notebook. It was the same time that I began "hearing" music for the Blake poems that I recorded. On the way home from Neal's funeral, I kept hearing lines from Blake's "Let the brothels of Paris be opened . . ."

P.P.: *Did you hear Blake's voice again?*

A.G.: Just the tune, a haunting tune. It's interesting that there were no drugs associated with the Blake visions. That's sort of nice. It gives another dimension. Different dimensions: that's the crux of my whole search (or my whole confusion!).

P.P.: *The drug quest and the Blake visions overlap, in my view, with the great themes of death, which is certainly one of the major motifs of your work.*

A.G.: Yes, but a lot of people don't recognize that. Actually, it's more a *fear* of death—unfortunately. Maybe that's why people don't want to recognize it, a very good reason, perhaps. The death visions I had back then were a mystery to me. In fact, I never did figure it out, except that it was like a sudden sensation of total suffering, a feeling of the ego being completely squashed out, smothered out. Annihilation.

P.P.: *I remember you saying it was too much to bear at one point.*

A.G.: Yeah, it was scary. I thought that if I continued that my head might explode, that I might have a brain seizure, a heart attack.

P.P.: *Your Blake visions, though, did become one of the major foundations for your poems, indirectly and directly. In fact, you said the other day that the Blake visions made you get off on the wrong track for at least fifteen or twenty years.*

A.G.: Well, that's a good way of characterizing it. I actually believed that ordinary reality, sometime, could be replaced by the vastness of my vision reality—a glimpse of a reality so brief

115

that it seemed another mode. But, maybe ordinary consciousness slowly encompasses death—in a very subtle way, a very slow, creeping way. It might even be like the renunciation of nirvana, which is the same as nirvana, which is an idea, which is the original perception of samsara and nirvana—or time and eternity. The terms become identical. Time is eternity, eternity is time, which is a known verbal formula: form is emptiness, emptiness is form. Time is eternity, eternity is time. Time is no different from eternity, eternity is no different from time. I wasn't smart enough to think of that formula. That is why I like Buddhism, because Buddhism does provide the mental formulas for recognizing and categorizing that kind of experience and working with it. And, it teaches to not get hung up on something for fifteen or twenty years, maybe even to forget it.

P.P.: *Since the early 1970's you've been involved with Tibetan Buddhism, devoting yourself to daily meditation sittings— even spending two or three months at a time doing nothing else but traditional Buddhist meditation. Have you ever tried long meditation under the influence of mind-expanding drugs, like acid.*

A.G.: I've combined sitting [meditation] and grass quite a bit. Sitting and acid? Yes, yes I have, come to think of it—a couple of times. The last time was 1972 when I did acid in the Teton mountains. I sat most of the day meditating—probably about six hours or so. The first three hours I was hung up trying to write an advertisement for the Snow Lion Inn. I got all tangled up in my prose qualities, somewhat frustrated. So I went up to the top of the mountain and just sat on a rock for four or five hours. I experienced complete tranquility that time.

P.P.: *That sounds a long way from your initial acid experiences, the one's I've seen recorded in your notebooks and the ones you published in "Kaddish," where you frequently had horrendous battles with the realization, the painful awareness of bodily and universal death.*

A.G.: Yeah, that's completely different. By this time, the acid trip is completely tranquil, empty and tranquil. During the Teton acid-meditation experience, I paid attention to my breath, in the Tibetan meditation style. The attention to breath combined with the acid was a very beautiful combination, very much the visual image of sitting in some high mountain in the midst of a giant mandala. So that Teton trip was a relatively empty trip, a tripless trip compared with the demons and fear I experienced on those trips in the late sixties. But the Teton experience always had a back brain telephone ring of the awareness of having taken acid. The ideal of LSD is complete absorption in present space. I had to settle for just empty space, since I had had so many ugly visions and didn't want to chase after those any more. So, I was willing to settle for empty space in front of me, on acid or off acid. I mean that the fear of the Lord or fear of karma or fear of disillusion, or fear itself was annihilated by the acceptance of emptiness. So, the funny part is that, in a sense, acid cancels itself—unless, as Gregory Corso says, it shows you more of what isn't there.

P.P.: *I have practiced all day meditation while sitting on acid. I experienced a complete sense of "hereness," an absolute feeling of just being. Yet, after about five or six hours, I began to sense a self-consciousness that I was just tripping out. That self-consciousness annihilated the previous experience completely. Then, instead of focusing on my breath and the here and now, I became transfixed by my fear of losing that consciousness. Somehow it was connected to a consciousness of death, that, ultimately, the body dies and there isn't any breath, any here and now—there is only emptiness.*

A.G.: Well, paying attention to the breath wipes out that self-consciousness. I would say meditation is above acid, ultimately. I must admit it. I was wrong all along.

P.P.: *But you used acid as a means of exploring consciousness. Naturally, it led to a breakdown of sorts, but even that is a great lesson. The freak-out acid poems you recorded in the late 1950's are really different from the acceptance of everything attitude you display in the acid poem, "Wales Visitation."*

A.G.: That experience was another example of meditative

breath and acid. I finally took a trip where I wasn't freaked out. I was sitting cross-legged in the soft grass, mind motionless, breath trembling by the white daisies by the roadside. It was the first time I'd taken acid in years, maybe four or five years. Most of the times I had taken it previously—it was just like grass—it scared me, made me tremble. So I'd gone off acid for a couple years because it made me tremble. I was feeling somewhat cowardly and hypocritical during that time because—this was during the mid-sixties—even though I wasn't taking acid, I was asking for its legalization. Not only was I not taking it because of the fear of a trembling trip, but because of the fear of being busted, the paranoia of being busted because the situation created by the police made it hard to get high.

P.P.: *That's not really paranoia—it's a clear perception of the police. Paranoia is an abnormal state of mind where what you fear is actually nonexistent.*

A.G.: No, it's not paranoia, but it's a kind of paranoia deliberately created by police agencies—as they've boasted of doing (like the FBI). A positive aspect of this situation was the contact with the police state that so many of us felt. I think acid and grass sensitized people to contact with the police state, and, in particular, that those changed in consciousness were somewhat under control of the state. That was a shocking thing to discover, that the state was controlling consciousness! During many of my own acid trips, I'd be high and see this big giant network of electricity state consciousness. "Blue television light seems to part my windows across the moonless tenement backyard." I started seeing dragons and serpent monsters. I had to stop taking acid.

P.P.: *But something must have happened, changed, to allow you to have such an idyllic trip as recorded in your "Wales Visitation" poem.*

A.G.: Well, by then (1967) I had sort of calmed down, looked over the situation, and realized that it was time to relax a little. Also, there was one other thing—a Tibetan Nyingma teacher, Dujom Rinpoche, told me "If you see anything horrible, don't

cling to it. And if you see anything beautiful, don't cling to it."
And by seeing anything horrible, it meant to me to stop
clinging to the vomit serpent hallucinations I had seen on LSD.
Some of those acid trips were like a touching of a reptilian
consciousness which Burroughs has written about very well. I
actually saw the universe as a vast serpent or dragon, a slow
moving dragon. There's several registers of that kind of
experience. One time at Tim Leary's house, I was high on
psilocybin—didn't you read that account in my uncollected
work—?

P.P.: *I remember reading two accounts of bad acid trips, one
where people you knew turned into demons.*

A.G.: Yeah, I remember being seated like a seraph king or
something, surrounded by the "reptile Devas of my Karma,"
meaning Peter [Peter Orlovsky, Ginsberg's longtime friend and
companion], who looked like a reptile. We were in the garden of
Eden, and he was some kind of Eve reptile. It was hard to
reassure him of my good intentions. He went through a lot of
shit with me because I kept getting scared.

P.P.: *I remember reading an interview with you conducted in
England sometime in 1965. Your attitudes toward acid at that
time were somewhat mixed. I guess it had something to do
with your visions of monsters and demons?*

A.G.: I was still dubious then about my relationship to acid. I
expressed it in the interview—but shortly thereafter, I took
another trip. I was in Big Sur, at Lawrence Ferlinghetti's cabin.
It was a very open trip, and I used much of it to sort of stabilize
myself. I had done some mantra chanting by then, maybe even
some meditation—enough so that my nature had calmed
somewhat, and I was a lot more secure. I also was a lot less
interested in seeing serpent faces in the clouds, more interested
in just seeing natural objects. I wasn't looking to acid for an
eternity outside of time. I wasn't looking for an eternal face in
the trees. I was just looking at the "time trees."

P.P.: *I remember you telling me about that trip. Weren't you,
at that time, getting pretty involved with the peace move-*

ment, as well as worried about the people of Viet Nam?

A.G.: I was thinking a lot about the peace movement and the Vietnam peace marches of those years. I remember getting down on my knees on the beach and praying for Johnson because he was going into the operating room to get a gall bladder operation. I realized the more vituperation and aggression there was in the air from me and others, even in thought, the more paranoid he was going to be when he got out from under the operation. They wouldn't learn anything if he just returned to a world of angry, paranoid illusions—and they would murder more in Vietnam. So I remember getting down and praying for Johnson's health. Later on, after the acid trip, I wrote a note to the magazine where the interview was published saying that I had revised my views—as of the interview—and wanted to calm whatever anxiety I created about the role of acid and how I thought it was a good thing for clarifying mind. I mentioned a few images about my praying for Johnson, praying for Peter whom I'd seen dancing naked on the beach in the sense of a vast space eternal seashore. That was the time when *I finally got over bum trips.*

P.P.: *Sometime later, didn't you testify in Congress supporting acid?*

A.G.: In 1966, before the Dodd Judiciary Subcommittee on Juvenile Delinquency, I repeated some of my revelations about Johnson and my acid trip; I actually prepared a testimony including descriptions of praying for Johnson's health and saying that it seemed to me that acid, in a sense, had catalyzed a workable, viable, noble and pacifist attitude toward the peace movement, or within the peace movement, and that acid was a usable thing. I recommended that everyone take it, especially those in the government. That testimony was a result of that acid trip.

P.P.: *Wasn't the Big Sur acid experience the first time you'd ever taken acid out in nature?*

A.G.: Yeah, I think it was the first trip I took in nature—total nature. The next acid-nature trip was in Wales and is recorded in the poem "Wales Visitation" that we were talking about. The Wales experience involved a little mantra chanting, some sitting—watching my breath, somewhat in the Zen style. Any time I felt a sense of mental unbalance or destabilization or that "cosmic, demonic terror," I would just sit there on the hillside. But, I was still projecting—plasmacizing—the whole scene and projecting my breath onto the cosmos, comparing the heavens and the air and the atmosphere over England and over the valley to an ocean tide slowly moving. Then I compared that same breath that came out of my body with the air that soughed through the trees.

P.P.: *The Wales acid experience also helped you overcome other problems, didn't it?*

A.G.: Yeah, that trip solved the big problem I had always had about writing on acid, a psychological problem. It had always seemed that *observation impeded function*—in the sense that the desire to write a tremendous visionary poem on acid always plunged me into self-conscious hell. I felt that because I had a fixed idea, perhaps a totally passive, inert state of consciousness while in a state of acid vision, that it seemed contradictory to write. Or, that writing seemed to interrupt the compendium of multitudinous detail noticed in the acid visionary state. I always had trouble writing while on acid, as in my "Mescaline" and "Lysergic Acid" poems—which were records of bum trips. The bum trip seemed connected somewhat with the self-conscious stereotyping of myself as a poet writing. In other words, I was still looking for a vision, trying to superimpose the acid vision on the old memory of a cosmic-consciousness, or to superimpose an old memory on the acid vision—so that I was not living in the present time, not noticing so much of what was in front of me. You can pick up this dilemma in another poem, "Magic Psalm."

P.P.: *It seems in that poem, as well as others, that you were trying to overcome your attempt to merge with the abstract cosmic and, instead, just accept the cosmic in the particulars of everyday existence.*

121

A.G.: Yeah. In "Wales Visitation" I guess what I had come to was a realization that me making noise as poetry was no different from the wind making noise in the branches. It was just as natural. It was a *very important point.* The fact that there were thoughts flowing through the mind is as much of a natural object as is the milky way floating over the Isle of Skye. So, for the first time, I didn't have to feel guilt or psychological conflict about writing while I was high. Also, for the first time I was able to exteriorize my attention instead of dwelling on the inner images and symbols and keeping my eyes closed.

P.P.: *The quality of mind that you were able to perceive, then, with the aid of the acid, was paying attention to natural detail, instead of fighting an abstract demon in the soul?*

A.G.: Yeah, and the most telling of the details is the line

> "...of the satanic thistle that raises its horned symmetry
> flowering above sister grass-daisies' pink tiny
> bloomlets angelic as lightbulbs—"

That is practically microscopic observation of detail. It occurred to me that I could do this sort of thing by turning my eyes outside of my head and stop trying to reproduce my Blake visions of cosmic consciousness, which was subtly and truly there behind it all. But, on this acid trip, I finally found the path or the technique or the way to direct my attention outside of myself—so that I wasn't shaken by any made-up cosmological snakes or serpents. All I had to do was see what was in front of me! The Wales trip was the first time there were no heavy judgments to be made—it's just open consideration of the reality in front of me. The Big Sur trip was still tinged with a heaviness of political judgments to be made. In terms of my poetics, I finally embraced the objectivist viewpoint, if it means thoughts in the head can be described without subjective paranoia.

P.P.: *How much of your breakthrough can be attributed to taking acid in the country, in nature, as opposed to the city?*

A.G.: Well, with the absolute presence of electronic heavy metal paranoia, (and if you have a wobbly mind) the obvious

122

place to go is out of the city. However, I would be interested now in taking trips in the city and seeing the city as nature. It would be nice to not resent or be scared of the city. I'd like to try it. But the difficulty is still hangovers and memories of using it as an occasion for a poem. In fact, I'm feeling kind of creepy about taking acid trips just for poems, because it creates a kind of funny little aesthetic acid universe that seems separated from everyday ordinary mind.

P.P.: *So far, we've discussed your consciousness exploration via drugs in terms of grass, LSD, and morphine. How about peyote? I remember you saying that you took a peyote trip at your family's house in the early 1950's, sometime before you came out West and wrote "Howl."*

A.G.: That first peyote trip is published in a small magazine, *Birth,* and reprinted in an anthology of drug experiences, *The Drug Experience* [*The Drug Experience,* edited by David Eben, (N.Y.: Orion Press, 1961)]. It was a very pleasant trip— auspicious, neither heaven or hell. I got hung up a little bit on the phonograph playing some mombo music, Tito Puente, I think.

P.P.: *How in the hell did you get peyote in the early 1950's?*

A.G.: There was a store on the lower East Side, right off Second Avenue, near St. Mark's Church, which had it in the window—barrels full of magic from Laredo! There was even a live peyote plant in the window. It was a little magic shop run by a fat, funny fellow whom I never quite understood or trusted.

P.P.: *Not many people realize that much of your poem "Howl" was written with the aid of peyote. Can you talk about that a bit?*

A.G.: It was in San Francisco, on Nob Hill in an apartment of mine that I had when I was working in market research. I remember seeing the Sir Francis Drake Hotel roof as a sort of robot Moloch face—that was the first peyote trip there. Then, I think there was a second trip with Peter [Orlovsky]. That was a very interesting trip. I looked into Peter's eyes, and I couldn't find anyone there. He looked into mine and couldn't find anyone there. There was a total absence, a vacancy and emptiness. After a year or two of building up a total romance with each other, it was a shock when we looked at each other and perceived two phantom ghosts with empty eyes, laughing fiendishly. I got scared, thinking "Oh, oh, it's all empty." I didn't know how to accept that then. I think that was the occasion I took the Powell street cable car and went down over Knob Hill down into the heart of the electric city under the Sir Francis Drake Hotel, muttering "Moloch, Moloch." So, I began writing the Moloch section of "Howl" while I was high, on the cable car under the Drake Hotel. I sketched out the rhythmic refrain, "Moloch whose eyes are a thousand blind windows ..." etc. I think I got the word Moloch from the movies, probably Fritz Lang or someone like that—some European 1930's expressionist film. "Howl" is an expressionist vision, so to speak.

P.P.: *So peyote was another one of those monstrous visions ...*

A.G.: Well, "monstrous" in the sense of laying my vision on society—on the cosmos. The next drug I used—it was 1958, I think—was some mescaline which I brought back to New York from Chicago for me, Peter, and Gregory [Corso].

P.P.: *You've published, in the book* Kaddish and Other Poems, *your mescaline trip, the poem entitled "Mescaline."*

A.G.: Yeah, it was written while I was high on mescaline, in New York, at my desk on 170 E. 2nd Street. One of the problems was the difficulty of writing well. The consciousness of writing imposes the need to make some great experience out of it, some visionary extraordinary experience. This creates an anxiety, a desire to make it be a heavenly god experience ...

P.P.: *The cosmic divine quest ...*

A.G.: Yeah, cosmic divine or demonic—whatever. Striving for cosmic sensations while at the same time straight vibrations and a desire for release and a fear of total release from the body. I had the *Tibetan Book of the Dead* by my side—not only then but in Peru when I took Ayahuasca, as well as when I took some in New York ...

P.P.: *You gave some Ayahuasca to Jack Kerouac as well.*

A.G.: Yeah. There was one very interesting experience with psilocybin during that time. Going to the bathroom and staring at the bathroom floor while taking a shit. The floor was a sort of dazzling mosaic tile, almost transparent, floating in space, floating world, and a feeling I could be in or out of my body. It didn't make any difference at the time. It was sort of funny, sort of charming—everything was so empty, it made me feel a sensation of charm, sweetness, dearness.

P.P.: *Sounds a lot mellower than the record of your Ayahuasca trips in 1960 in Peru [recorded in* The Yage Letters, *City Lights, 1963].*

A.G.: In Peru, I was appealing for some kind of blinding vision, destruction, dissolution, but in a grotesque, humorous way. The best record of that experience is in the poem "Magic Psalm." After the experience I wrote some notes for a poem, "The Reply," in my brujo's, my cuarandero's house. I remember I was sitting near some big gas tanks, near a jungle with a lot of mosquitoes.

P.P.: *We've covered a lot of your psychedelic experiments, most of them really, with the exception of laughing gas. There is, of course, at least two poems that come directly out of aether-laughing gas trips.*

A.G.: Laughing gas? I tried some before I went on down to South America. I was getting my teeth fixed by my cousin in New Jersey. He knew I was a poet, so I asked him to give me as much as he could. He was interested in his own way. So, he did a lot of experimenting in putting me out and bringing me up—putting me out under the threshold, turning on less oxygen. I had a notebook in my lap and would take notes as long as I was conscious—up to the point I would lose consciousness. The last thing that seems to leave is sound consciousness. I would wake up and record that if I could.

P.P.: *Was your primary motive still in search of a cosmic consciousness?*

A.G.: Yeah, and there, it seems to me, the whole point was that the total enlargement of consciousness is *oblivion!* There

125

would be no separate individuation any longer. Actually, it's a blanking out of the senses, rather than an enlargement of the senses because, one by one, the senses go out under laughing gas. It gives the appearance of enlarging perception to a point where the totality of the universe invades the individual entity and dissolves the individual entity into the blackness of space. But the moment you grasp it, you go out. So, the only thing you can appreciate is coming back and realizing that you've grasped it—and that what you've grasped is something ungraspable by the human form and consciousness. It kind of makes the human form a sort of joke. I saw it in Buddhist terms, in a manner of speaking. You'll remember I dedicated the poem "Laughing Gas" to the poet/Zen student Gary Snyder:

> *To Gary Snyder*
> The red tin begging cup you gave me
> I lost it but its contents are undisturbed.

Meaning that it was empty. Then, I remember writing a big long letter to Mark Van Doren [Ginsberg's professor at Columbia University, also a poet] reporting on my latest phases of investigation and saying that death was the mother of the universe, basically.

P.P.: *And your aether experience, that was in Peru, right?*

A.G.: Yeah. I had a whole bottle of aether by myself. I decided to take it continuously until the aether bottle was used up and just write continuously to see if I could pursue the figment of my cosmic search. Aether is very similar to laughing gas, practically the same as far as a sense of simultaneity of universes and oblivion of all universes cancelling themselves out. Or all consciousness cancelling itself out. There I was in Lima near a railroad station. It seemed clear that I was hearing a bell that would ring at this one time and never return. I thought that the universe might unfold and repeat itself again and that some day it would return to that very same moment, and I'd be sitting there with that rag of aether over my nose. That's Nietzsche's eternal return, a very definite impression of that.

P.P.: *Sounds frightening...*

A.G.: It was very awesome. Not entirely frightening, but I certainly felt trapped in a recurrent universe. Sort of like a science fiction recurrent universe with the added horror of realizing that by the time twenty-seven thousand million years went by, I'd have forgotten it all completely. But the weird thing was that on aether you seem to remember that it had happened before. So that this one bell was sounding once and never again and both, and it would be repeated also!

VIII

On Mantras

P.P.: *How did you ever manage to have a mellow psychedelic experience, after all the "awesome" cosmic episodes?*

A.G.: I guess the first good trip I had was in Bixby Canyon, high on acid while practicing mantra chanting. That's the trip I mentioned before—at Ferlinghetti's cabin in the country, Big Sur. I remember Neal [Cassady] was there. I was sitting on top of a rock combatting my fear of the scene and the acid by chanting a Japanese mantra against disasters. While I was chanting, Neal was passing by over a bridge in the distance in a car. He didn't want to spend the evening at the cabin. So I stayed home there sitting on a big rock in the middle of the beach near the bridge, chanting for Neal's safety. Then there was an acid trip at Millbrook, Leary's place. We'd all taken acid, and there was a big huge fellow, a Canadian broadcasting interviewer who also had taken some acid. He began freaking me out; I was afraid he would get violent—though he was a gentle man. So, in order to protect myself I started chanting *Hare Krishna.* It ended up with fifteen or twenty of us, high on acid, chanting various Hindu mantras. The effect was to calm the acid, calm the people, calm the whole situation. Incidentally, I think that was one of the first times I did any chanting with Ram Dass [Richard Alpert]. It was one of his first times at hearing mantra chanting. He was very good about it, very supportive.

P.P.: *So mantra chanting became a means of calming yourself during acid freakouts, as well as during normal everyday situations?*

A.G.: Yeah. I practiced more and more chanting, at poetry readings, political rallies, parties, even in my kitchen—chanting at speed freaks who were stealing my transistor radio! [Laughs] Chanting became a way of calming—not only during difficult acid trips—but also a way of centering myself. The mantras that I used at Millbrook and in Big Sur and other places were a reference point, a reliable, relatively benevolent safe reality to center on. However, I was still associating the mantra with some erotic spiritual Lawrencian opening. I thought that the opening of the chakras as a result of mantra chanting might be an opening of the empty eyes, the ass, the loins, the belly, the solar plexis, the throat and head. Something out of Whitman, maybe, the opening of a love feeling. I was chasing love too much. I wanted love to be the end of the universe. I was looking for love to conquer all, rather than emptiness to conquer everything. I had misidentified love with *sunyatta.*

P.P.: *So the initial mantra singing was still . . .*

A.G.: Amatory. Also, it led to contact with the Shivananda lineage, with Swami Bhaktivedanta who gave me a long explanation of *Raja* Yoga. I realized then that I had to learn to give up, rather than indulging myself totally. I tried practicing breathing and mind control, but I never got very far with Shivananda's version.

P.P.: *After Bhaktivedanta, you met Swami Muktananda?*

A.G.: Yes. He gave me some good mantras and some sitting exercises. I began formal sitting [meditation] with him. The first three or four days of sitting is recorded in the poem "Guru Om." It represents the notes I took on a three day retreat in a motel in Dallas, where he was staying. He invited me to come

129

down with him. He gave me sitting instructions, and suggested I sit in my room. The great thing about Muktananda is the conversations I had with him about visions. I was sitting with him, holding his hand. We looked into each other's eyes. I was waiting for some zap, some electricity, and kept looking into his eyes. The feeling was, more or less, well balanced, not challenging—you know, hoping for something but at the same time curious, inquisitive. Then I noticed he was revolving his jaws with empty eyes. It was the same perception I had had on acid looking into the eyes of a lamb [recorded in "Wales Visitation"]. His eyes were empty. He wasn't laying a trip on me. He was empty. *That* was the nature of enlightenment, not having any particular thoughts in mind, not laying an aggressive trip on someone. It was an enormous relief.

P.P.: *What mantras did he give you?*

A.G.: *Guru Om*, which focuses on the breast, in the heart area. He also taught me a very beautiful version of the Shiva mantra, which I adapted with chords. Later, Trungpa suggested that I not sing it, though, because it was laying a trip on people—in a sense of raising a certain expectation which couldn't be satisfied by further teachings. You know what I mean. You do it for half an hour and finally everybody's tingling. You actually get a kundalini tingle. Trungpa felt it was too trippy, which I felt was true.

P.P.: *You were using mantras as a way of getting people into altered states of consciousness?*

A.G.: Well, first of all, mantras made good show biz! [Laughs] Also, I got some messianic notion of bringing chanting to America. It seemed so beautiful that it was worth doing. I saw it as a way of opening up an audience. I also saw it was a way of self-expression; it was a way of measuring breath—an old poetic technique. It was also a good way of sacramentalizing the occasion and bringing it to a serious tone to combat any kind of beatnik-beer-whisky-rowdy materialism. I began chanting mantras a lot at poetry readings back in 1963, in Vancouver, as soon as I had arrived from Japan. I used finger cymbals at that time. I can remember the first or second night I

130

was there. I went to a party and started chanting *Hare Krishna* with everyone joining in. That was the first time I'd tried that. Sometime later that week, Robert Duncan said that I seemed to use more of my body and my voice in chanting than I did while reading my poems, which I made a note of. And Swami Bhaktivedanta kept telling me to sing *Hare Krishna* (a couple of years later) after he had heard me singing it. So, I felt an official encouragement to sing.

P.P.: *Did you ever have any kind of visionary experience while or after chanting?*

A.G.: Yes, in 1968, in Chicago, during the Democratic convention. Once again, I used chanting as a way of calming myself down, of calming others, of creating a circle of empty aggression.

P.P.: *So mantras became a link from the bad acid trip to the good acid trip and then to further spiritual quests?*

A.G.: Yes, chanting finally became a link to yoga and to meditation. It is also linked to experiments in my poetry, experiments like "Hum Bom!" A lot of variations and developments with my Blake songs, my whole entering into music. My development with music began with mono-chordal chanting. After learning my first chord, I then went on to learn two and three chords which eventually evolved into putting Blake to music, as well as putting my own improvisations to music. First I would improvise the music, write or improvise the lyrics. That led to a long poem written with music simultaneously, "September on Jessore Road." So the chanting evolved into forms of song and entered into the poetry and into the verse structure.

P.P.: *Exactly how does mantra enter into the verse structure?*

A.G.: Mantra led to singing, singing led to song! I became even more aware of the emphasis on some particular articulation of the vowels. I always was interested in breath, as you know—as in "Howl." But, chanting made me conscious of the role of breath. I wasn't quite so conscious of it as a living continuous quality, which was like a basic, a great reference point. I didn't

131

realize how much (when I wrote "Howl") a long breath was necessarily a great reference point to reality—or the awareness of breath.

P.P.: *I remember you telling me that your song "Don't Smoke" was actually based on Australian aborigine chants.*

A.G.: Yes, that's right, "Don't Smoke" is actually based on the Australian aborigine chanting rather than the Oriental. Oddly enough, 'the record made in the Columbia Studios of that sounds like a weird amplification of many of the elements of authentic song-man village chants. I was able to sing *Hare Krishna* to the Australian aborigines, and they were able to sing it back. We were able to trade chants! They had a great auditory imagination and memory so that they could chant *Hare Krishna* once or twice and be able to continue. Several of their song-men could do that. I even put on an evening of chanting with Australian aborigines, in which I was doing Buddhist and Hindu chants and they were doing aboriginal chants. I was chanting theirs, they were chanting mine. I have recordings of aboriginal chanting, and I have some books on it. I added that in as a sort of poetics.

P.P.: *Are you still doing much chanting [1976]?*

A.G.: Not as much. When I'm alone at readings, I do lots of chanting or singing. I always try to chant at a poetry reading, try to begin with a chant. It sets the stage, calms the scene, spreads some dharma, and sets a level where everybody can be. It relaxes my voice, prepares my voice, prepares my mind. While chanting I have a chance to look over the pretty boys in the audience [laughs], to become conscious of the space in the room. I don't have to look down on the page; I can look out into the audience and establish some kind of eyeball contact with the people while I'm chanting.

P.P.: *Is that a kind of surrendering, in a way, surrendering to the space around you—in Trungpa's sense?*

A.G.: Yes, surrendering to the inevitability of the night or day and seeing other people there. Over the years, I've used a lot of different chants. In the seventies, I've evolved a lot of activity

132

chanting *Om Mani Padme Hum* which I learned from Tarthang Tulku. He suggested I go out and sing that mantra and one other *(Om Ah Hum Vajra Padma Siddhi Hum)*. Two years later, after singing them a great deal and getting sort of a huge vibe out of it, Trungpa suggested I not use them because they were putting me and the audience into a sort of suspended trance state, arousing us into high vibes. But, having no follow up (there was no meditation to follow it up, nothing to nail it down) it was like putting them on a trip. What he suggested was *Ah* and *Gate Gate Paragate* . . . and the address to the human Buddha. For a long while I did the *Prajna Paramita Sutra* in Japanese and in English. I developed that for quite a while. I checked it out in 1967 with Roshi Suzuki and he said it was all right for me to record it.

IX

On Tibetan Buddhism

P.P.: *It seems that a lot of contemporary poetry struggles to ground itself in the bare facts of reality, but it's so hard to do—to clamp the mind down on the quotidian American world.*

A.G.: The difficulty is in the thinking. You're getting down to the bare facts of reality, but it's *not* the bare facts of reality— it's the bare facts of your own perceptions of reality. You can paint your perceptions, like the whole point of the war poetry I wrote: it wasn't about the war, it was about television and radio—war as seen, as represented on television, radio, and newspapers. I wasn't faking the subject (except in a few spots) because I was recording my reaction to the *electronic war,* the electronic images of war. It would have been a fake to enter into the battle imaginatively, actually there in the mud (which I do a couple of times in a line like "sensitive yellow boy by a muddy wall"), but mostly it's just a recording of the headlines or the TV thing. There's a journal note I had on Kennedy's death in a book called *Poetry and Power.* It's just a journal fragment, recording the imagery of the television screen recording his death, rather than as if I were in Dallas. I was in

San Francisco looking at the TV. His death was being recorded on the blips of the screen, in a helicopter rising into the dot screen of television. In other words, it's not reporting on reality—unless you want to define reality as *what we see,* purely subjective. But, we *can* know what we see. We can't know reality, but we can know what we see. So that makes it easy: all you have to do is report what you actually see—not mind thoughts about what you see, but what you see directly, or hear directly. That makes it like rolling off a log. You don't have to delve and analyze for reality. All you have to do is be aware of what you just saw.

P.P.: *Sounds somewhat like the Tibetan sitting practices, the* samatha *and* vipasyana *meditation exercises. You've been seriously meditating in this tradition since 1971 or 1972, haven't you?*

A.G.: I sat a year and a half first (I think 1970-71) with eyes closed *Guru Om* mantra for Muktananda. Then, in 1972, I think Trungpa suggested shifting to a more complex mantra, but with eyes open, a mantra without associations: *A, Ah, Sha, Sa, Ma, Ha*—representing the six worlds of Bardo, I think, as well as six chakras. But, with the eyes open, and on the out-breath only. Then, when I went in 1973 to the three month meditation Naropa seminary . . .

P.P.: *In Wyoming?*

A.G.: Yeah. He switched everybody within different kinds of advanced or *samatha* meditation just to the simple *samatha*—no mantra, eyes open, outbreath. I've been doing that ever since.

P.P.: *Could you explain what the* samatha *practice is?*

A.G.: I've heard it defined—*samatha,* a Sanskrit word—as pacification of mind, or calming of mind, or tranquilization of mind style. Just the other day, Trungpa defined it as wakefulness, a step toward wakefulness. Mindfulness. Wakefulness or mindfulness, as well as *samatha* also in the direction of tranquilization of thought or making thought more and more transparent and less and less solidified and obsessive. The more

135

and more conscious and transparent the thought forms that pass, the less attachment to the thought forms; but there is more observation of their nature and character. That leads to what is called *vipasyana*, which is insight into detail, or awareness of detail. First, mindfulness, then, awareness around—particularly in the space around. The practice itself consists in sitting in the usual meditation posture with a tripod base, crosslegged, if possible, to give a good solid firm base, grounded to earth, straight spine. According to Suzuki Roshi, ears in line with the shoulders, nose in line with the belly button, top of the head upholding heaven. Specifically, *samatha*—as distinct from Zen style—is paying attention to the breath leaving the nostril and dissolving into the space in front of the face, or the space around—in front of you. I've heard it described as sort of like touch and let go, touch and let go, touch and let go—or attention to the breath going out, and then dropping it as the breath ceases, and then attention again to the breath when it goes out. So it's practice in *re*directing your attention constantly to the space in front of your face, outside of your body. In that sense, almost by definition of practice, of egolessness because you're meditating on the empty space into which your breath dissolves, rather than into any psychological or sensational phenomena going on inside the body. Then there is a constant daydreaming and drifting away from that attention to the space. You're constantly waking up—mindfully waking up to the actual space around you, into which you're breathing. You use the breath as a handle to get back into that space.

P.P.: *So, you've been doing these practices since 1972?*

A.G.: Yeah, a variety of it since 1972, and then strictly empty *samatha*—just breath, outbreath *samatha*—since 1973. Sometimes very intense practice, like at the seminary ten to twelve hours a day for weeks at a time. I've gone on various meditation retreats of two weeks, or one week, or three weeks—each which involved sitting ten hours a day, practicing that. I've done it enough to be proceeding on to a more complicated series of exercises.

P.P.: *Tantric exercises?*

A.G.: I think they're classified as tantric. I think they're called preliminary practices for tantra—getting the body in shape, prostrations . . .

P.P.: *Can you explain what prostrations are? Do you do visualizations as well?*

A.G.: Yes, I do prostrations . . . Visualizations of the lineage of teachers and the various attendant images and symbols of divinities and aspects of Buddha, or aspects of mind. And some mantra repetition, involving the refugees. It's sort of like the prostrations occupy the body, and the mantra repetition occupies the speech, and visualization occupies the mind. You get all three going at once, like whirling prayer wheels, three prayer wheels simultaneously. Not necessarily in relation to each other because they're all going on independently; all these three practices are what they call *Ngo-dro* or preliminary foundation practices. They are very interesting because they're Blakean, involving concentration on the visualization—building a slow practice, and building up a visual picture in the mind, rationally or in a rational orderly way . . .

P.P.: *It's like William Blake visualizing a picture on a completely blank page—the mind-imagination transposed to an empty page . . .*

A.G.: Yeah, and the procedure is very beautiful. It doesn't involve, you know, having to do anything special, except to memorize directions; then you visualize those flashes in different parts of feet and hair and clothes, and just build up the picture over a period of months and months as you're doing the prostrations. It's sort of like the *samatha* and *vipasyana* are for the purpose of clearing the mind, making the thoughts more transparent—so that there's not a lot of garbage there obstructing the later practices. Once you've cleared the ground, so to speak, you've got your mind opened up, relaxed. Then you can proceed to build houses in your head. Whereas, if you were to try and do it—if you were obsessed with sex or with gods or drugs or poetry or anything . . .

P.P.: *Or mind, or thought...*

A.G.: Or mantras... that would be an obstruction. You'd constantly refer to that instead of having wiped the slate clean and building up the picture. So, the practices are good training for poetry, in a sense.

P.P.: *There's a long, powerful lineage of Tibetan and Zen poets that developed their work out of their meditation practices. Have you spent much time reviewing that tradition?*

A.G.: Yes. I've read a great deal in the Tibetan tradition, *The Royal Song of Saraha*, various poetic books like the lives of Naropa and sGam.po.pa (*The Jewel Ornament of Liberation*), Trungpa's poetry, various scattered texts, Tilopa's address to Naropa, etc.

P.P.: *What do you think about Trungpa's approach to meditation?*

A.G.: The Tibetan monks I've talked to all report that Trungpa's meditation is very good. His teaching of meditation is excellent: acute, practical, experienced—he seems to know all the angles. From his own experience, he's gone to the center and is able to teach it well. He said some amazing things to me, like I was hung up on where does my breath begin and end. I went through it very early, and he gave me the image of the breath continuing, sort of, from one breath to another like an opening up of a telescope. Beautiful. I mean one breath leading to another, like the unfolding or opening up of a telescope. Very beautiful, precise image, and once I thought of it in those terms, it seemed to resolve a psychological-mental bind I had, or a self-consciousness I had, in proceeding from one breath to another.

P.P.: *But you've always been concerned with breath, much longer than you've been studying in the Tibetan tradition...*

A.G.: Yes, that's true, it was implicit in the long line poems, like "Howl."

P.P.: *Has it changed, the poetics of breath, since you've been practicing* samatha, *etc.?*

138

A.G.: No, because poetry, poetic practice is sort of like an independent carpentry that goes on by itself. I think, probably, the meditation experience just made me more and more aware of the humor of the fact that breath is the basis of poetry and song—it's so important in it as a measure. Song is carried out on the vehicle of the breath, words are carried out through the breath, which seems like a nice "poetic justice." [Laughs] That the breath should be so important in meditation as well as in poetics. I think that must be historically the reason for the fact that all meditation teachers are conscious of their spoken breath, as poets are. That's the tradition, the *Kägu* tradition, that the teachers should be poets. And, that's the reason for the Naropa Kerouac School of Disembodied Poetics; originally, Trungpa asked me to take part in the school because his motive was that he wanted his meditators to be inspired to poetry because they can't teach unless they're poets—they can't communicate.

P.P.: *In the tradition of Milarepa . . .*

A.G.: Or any tradition, really: sharp, acute, flavorful communication.

P.P.: *What is the influence on your recent poetry of your dedication to the* samatha-vipasyana *practice? For example, in terms of the focus of attention, the ability to actually see, record, etc., how the mind operates, as well as becoming conscious of your perceptions of the quotidian world . . .*

A.G.: It's more in the area of observing the mechanical nature of certain passions, like anger and sex, so that they become more transparent. I get less entrapped in them, like political anger—it affects me politically. One thing Trungpa said when I was yelling at him for smoking and drinking was that any trip I lay on him proceeds from my own anxiety and creates more anxiety in him. And so does not resolve the problem, but increases the problem.

P.P.: *So, his instructions had an effect on your political . . .*

A.G.: Well, it had an effect on my entire political strategy. I had the same lesson with my father. The more I attacked my father, the more I drove him into a wall, so that he wouldn't oppose the war until one day I heard him arguing against the war and taking my side with someone else. I realized that the argument I had with my father had nothing to do with the war. It was a wall of frustration between us. In order to get my father to really oppose the war, I had to soften down and talk about it reasonably, without attacking him, without animosity. I just had to really reconsider the whole thing, present my facts in an orderly way, in a way that he could understand and receive without it offending his ego. That's pious, skillful means, I suppose, but that depends on curbing your anger and being able to communicate what you know. When you're shouting and angry, you don't really communicate the details of what you know. Very often you mistake opposition for evil, when it's misunderstanding.

P.P.: *But you still are writing political poetry, as I noticed going through your new manuscript, the one you are preparing for City Lights—what's it going to be called?*

A.G.: *"Mind Breaths"* maybe. Yes, I'm still writing political poetry.

P.P.: *One of the new poems, like "News Bulletin," for example, is political, but not in the raving, angry style of "Howl" or some of your other "angry" political things. It is not denying the obvious political problems, but, at the same time, it doesn't strive toward a heaviness, a hard-line. Is that an example of the different political consciousness?*

A.G.: Well, yes, sort of, because it's really a literal description of my reactions to the news, while simultaneously putting it in the poem as images. What I was actually doing—either about it or simultaneously, as I heard the different kinds of news—is I was comparing, realistically, my actual life with my news resentments.

> "Criminal possession of a controlled substance—
> Marijuana" just came over the radio
> and I got mad & sent Rockerfeller a
> crystal skull postcard.

140

In other words, I wasn't taking a partial account of just my resentments, my angers, and my perceptions of politics, but I was including what my real life was doing at the same time—sometimes contrasting with the so-called anger. In a sense, I was exposing my own hypocrisy, as well as the humor of the actual situation of getting angry, and, at the same time, making borscht [laughs]—which is natural. And unless there is that space, to include both minds, "both-mind," you can't deal realistically with the subject. You just have a single-edged, just a single-minded obsessional view, which excludes other people's activities—including your own. It's less accommodating. Total anger is less accommodating than a slightly larger perspective of awareness, which may move and change things. A larger perspective and awareness can actually change other people; whereas, accusation and guilt-strumming tend to solidify people in their behavior patterns. This is something I knew long ago, everybody knows—it's taken for granted. But, specifically, in that business about Johnson and the war—see, Johnson actually, as by hindsight we realize, was really quite bewildered by the whole scene in fact, sincere in a weird way. He quit, he gave up, which is bigger than anything anybody else did . . .

P.P.: *Actually, his resignation was unprecedented, remarkable in his own way . . .*

A.G.: Yeah, terrific on his part. The problem was that people really didn't communicate to him, they just yelled at him. I guess "Hey, hey, LBJ, how many kids did you kill today?" must have stung him. It would sting me if somebody outside of a poetry theatre were to say I wanted to fuck ass, fuck boys' asses. (I remember, once, a guy was handing out pamphlets saying "Don't listen to Ginsberg. All he wants to do is get young boys and fuck them in the ass." I was really stung by that, because it really hit home.) But that had to be followed, then, by some kind of communication of other facts to him, and it seemed he was imprisoned with a set of—he definitely was imprisoned with a set of facts and interpretations handed to him by his advisors which unbalanced his judgment. When, finally, Acheson and a whole bunch of other people got together and really laid the facts down on him—that he wasn't winning the war and that the reports from Westmoreland weren't true—his reason collapsed, his mind collapsed, and his whole structure collapsed. So he was collapsible. But the technique used to puncture his illusions was too violent and rhetorical, and, maybe, didn't include enough—I don't know, it wasn't soft enough. Nobody succeeded before '68, nobody succeeded in communicating to Johnson—at the cost of millions of lives!

P.P.: *So, getting back to meditation techniques, they help you . . .*

A.G.: Calm down, consider what would be the best way of communicating the simplest elements of facts—unprejudiced by my own anger and resentments. If you package your information in resentment and accusation, people won't swallow it as easily as if you package it in some kind of, or maybe even unpackaged, neutral, benevolent, indifferent attention. If you package it in attention, it's much better than if you package it in inattentive resentment. You're not taking into account the psychology of the other guy.

P.P.: *This sounds like the Buddhist stress on the aspect of compassion . . .*

A.G.: There is an element of compassion, but it isn't really compassion. It's really compassion toward yourself—that you're not tearing yourself apart, banging your head against the wall. I noticed that I kept all this accumulated newspaper clippings and material and would go into rages over them, but I never did anything about them. I mean, the amount I did about them was somehow inhibited by the enormity of the rage that I had. So I never was able to take clear actions, early, to present all my stuff about CIA dope, for example, in a reasonable form that people could get to . . .

P.P.: *Yeah, but what I meant was that in working with "the space around you," with the* vipasyana *technique in particular, you recognize that . . .*

A.G.: It's the by-product. Awareness is a by-product of that, because sitting at Naropa seminary, for say two weeks on end, ten hours a day, the same political resentments and outrages—like blood boiling and adrenalin rushes over Kissinger would rise, over and over again, until I found I was having my rages over Kissinger, Mitchell, occasionally, C.L. Solzberger of the *Times*—of all people!—and Victor Riezel, a labor columnist, and various other minor characters. I would get into these enormous towering rages over minor characters like Solzberger because they were some part of my culture system, and I realized that Solzberger wasn't worth getting angry over! You know—maybe Nixon or Kissinger, but Solzberger wasn't worth a rage as big as Kissinger.

P.P.: *So this poem "News Bulletin" reflects a new sense of compassion . . .*

A.G.: This poem? I wasn't using the word compassion. I think awareness is better. Compassion arises from awareness which rises from the realization that as I am trapped in my rage and blindness, other people are also trapped in their rage and blindness, and so they don't hear what's being said.

P.P.: *That's somewhat what I meant by compassion.*

A.G.: What I'm saying is that compassion is a by-product of an empty awareness. I would stress the *awareness* aspect, the insight and awareness aspect, rather than the compassion aspect. If you start with compassion, then you have to manufacture some kind of love heart out of nothing. Whereas compassion rises, it seems to rise of its own nature, without asking. Then you see things clearly, like a poor little doggie on the street. Okay, so you're busy with your poetry and the dog's yelp is irritating. But if you actually look at the situation and see the dog, you realize it doesn't have anything to do with your writing poetry. It is out there injured in the street! The question is, would there be a danger that such an awareness would vitiate activity, vitiate action, or vitiate practical action to relieve suffering? I don't think so. I don't think common sense can be harmful. I think . . . the colossal exemplification of that was the fact that all the outrage in Chicago, during the

143

Democratic Convention, woke a lot of understanding, and broke the crust and made a lot of people see the authoritarian government with more insight—and scared people of the police state. It also took the attention of the whole Democratic Party, and of Humphrey, at that time. Later historical records show that Humphrey really wanted to get rid of the war. And he was stuck with Johnson, but even Johnson, by then, wanted to get rid of the war too. But they weren't able to do it and not lose face, totally. The actual fact was that Johnson sent a message to Thieu saying that they were going to make peace before the election, so that Humphrey could benefit by that, just as Nixon did in '72. They were going to pose, more or less, the same peace treaty, a coalition government with the Viet Cong included. But Nixon and Mitchell sent Madame Chenault to Saigon to tell Thieu to hang on and not accept Johnson's deal because if Nixon came in, he'd keep them going. Now this was the cause that came out when, after all the wiretapping and bugging was revealed, the Republicans brought up that Johnson had been wiretapping and bugging Mrs. Chenault. Remember that? The reason was because of this political mission on her part. Now the radicals were so angry at the liberals and so outraged and self-righteous that they were thinking that the liberals were worthless. But the main issue was the war, they said, everybody's main issue was the war then and whether the war would be stopped. Certainly the Viet Cong in North Vietnam weren't interested in our anger at the liberals. They were interested in our stopping the war, and would have been better off with Humphrey. I think there's an example where a vast national hysterical anger passion may have, on the part of the left movement, may have actually prolonged the war, a prolongation of four or five years. There was an escalation of the war and more people were killed. There was more bombing and more damage done than in the *previous* years. So the unmindful anger loosed on Humphrey, plus the total resentment of the whole situation on the part of the left, led to conditions at the time of the election where youth stayed away and the radicals stayed away from the vote and Nixon squeaked in by a half million! He didn't win by much, he barely won. If the entire left had been, if not vociferously backing Humphrey, at least gone to the polls and voted him in, I think the war would have ended a lot earlier. Whether that in the long run would have been good or bad, I don't know either, because Watergate was a good show! We're lucky that we had Nixon for Watergate. But when you see the war went on . . . but maybe Watergate balanced that out. So, finally, who's right and who's wrong? Who has reason to be self-righteous and angry—finally?

P.P.: *That seems to demonstrate a tremendous change in your political consciousness . . .*

A.G.: Not too much. I was chanting *om* in Chicago. I voted for Humphrey. From 1966 on I had a pretty good insight into Johnson. And I had a poem about 1965, "Who Be Kind To," prayers for the ghost and demons. My consciousness is more refined now, but the basic insight was already there. Anyway, I always had it from Kerouac: "to avoid new reasons for spitefulness," that was his phrase. He saw Abbie Hoffman and Jerry Rubin as inventing new reasons for spitefulness. So I begin to deal with that problem in "Who Be Kind To":

> Be kind to the politician weeping in the galleries
>> of Whitehall, Kremlin, White House
>> Louvre and Phoenix City
> aged, large nosed, angry, nervously dialing
>> the bald voice connected to
> electrodes underground converging thru
>> wires vaster than a kitten's eye can see
> on the mushroom shaped fear-lobe under
>> the ear of Sleeping Dr. Einstein
> crawling with worms, crawling with worms, crawling
>> with worms the hour has come—
> Sick, dissatisfied, unloved, the bulky
>> foreheads of Captain Premier President
>> Sir Comrade Fear!

So it's characterizing them as being in a state of fear—unloved, out of contact, angry, nervous. There's a certain amount of awareness of their condition; I'm saying "Be kind to them. Be kind to the dictators." Which is pretty awful. That was in 1965, and in 1966 I went in front of Congress and talked about praying for Johnson's health, rather than piling more anxiety on him. I felt that the more anxiety piled on him, the more imprisoned and paranoid he would become—and the more damage that would be done. My correlation is the more he got yelled at in a blind, angry way, the more people would be killed in Vietnam. I think that's a relatively correct judgment. It means the situation is too dangerous for us to be angry.

P.P.: *And is this underscored by the Tibetan practices?*

A.G.: Yeah. Well, I mean life is too dangerous to get angry. The anger only comes back on yourself; also the anger only comes back on me—in the form of sickness, finally. All the anger I accumulated, I think was responsible for the illness I have had in the last few years. I had a really total object lesson in *that*, breaking my leg in 1971, I think it was.

P.P.: *Didn't you slip on some ice or something?*

A.G.: Yeah. I was up in Cherry Valley on the farm with Gregory. I was a little irritated at having to take care of him. Denise and the other people had left a lot of dogs around, and I was responsible for taking care of the dogs too. I don't like dogs that much. I didn't want to take care of more than one or two, and there were four or five. I had to keep interrupting my "poetic beauty" to go outside every day and take care of the dogs—feed them, water them. One really cold day, I went out to the barn where they were, to bring them food. I was carrying their water and food, but I was really irritated and angry—stomping out angrily, and I stomped right out on the ice and slipped and fell. As I was walking I was thinking—resentfully—"Why did they leave those dogs with me, rah rah rah . . ." So I wasn't watching where I was going. I wasn't being mindful of the fact that I had already slipped on the ice because of these slick tennis shoes I was wearing. I should have been slower and more deliberate and enjoyed what I was doing; or, at least, been aware of what I was doing, and put some good boots on to go out there on the slippery ice. Done it right; but, I thought, "Awh, fuck it, I'll get out there. I'll do it and get back here . . ." It was a direct object lesson that while the mind was clouded with resentment and anger, I could get hurt! I mean it was just totally direct. There was no way out. I just lay there on the ice, fallen down, having slipped on the ice while realizing something disastrous had happened. Also, I was seeing very clearly the chain of emotional events which led me to go and slip on the damn ice. It was no accident, in the sense that one of the conditioning factors of slipping was that I wasn't being careful where I was walking because I wasn't observing the ground since my eyes were rolled in my head in anger. It's just direct cause and effect, not an ideological matter. There was no way out, like Anne Waldman says, "No escape." So that's totally related to mindfulness practice.

P.P.: *So the meditations help create a general awareness of the outside world, the space around us, as well as the space inside, learning how to deal with emotions, become aware of the currents of feeling. Does that kind of awareness enter into your poetry practice?*

A.G.: Well, let's see. Yeah, I think so, because rather than settling for accusatory generalization, like "God damn finks!" I have to research my anger and find what was the original fact that I was thinking about and present that and see if that looks as bad as my "God damn fink!" epithet . . .

P.P.: *Or "God damn that fucking dog . . ."* [Laughs]

A.G.: [Laughs] Yeah. I have to really go back to the ground of the situation, get back to the fact and say what it is I'm resenting and write that down as an image. "Dogs barking in the barn calling for their food in the icy hay" or something like that. Is that something to get angry about? Otherwise, I might have said "Having to go out and feed the dirty dogs of reality" or something, rather than "the dogs lonesome in the barn barking in their icy hay." When you have to go back to the "icy hay" you come up with poetry. I mean the "icy hay" is much better than "dirty dogs." That's why I said, in "Broken Bone Blues":

> Broke my body like a dog
> Like a scared dog indeed
> Broke my dumb body . . .

147

P.P.: *So instead of writing abstract poetry coming out of an unconscious, unmindful energy, you are more concerned with writing poetry that is mindful in the* vipasyana *sense...*

A.G.: Well, my poetry was always pretty mindful anyway. I always had based it on elements of William Carlos Williams' elemental observations. Since I went through the same kind of crisis in having an abstracted, visionary experience and clinging to that in abstract forms and then having to take refuge in Williams' "No ideas but in things" back in '53 ... so I've gone through a lot of cycles of the same ...

P.P.: *Realization...*

A.G.: Different aspects and closer and closer to the known, closer and closer to my own life. How it affects it is—instead of having a generalization rising out of the anger, a sort of surrealist image, you get an even better surrealist image if you go back to the lonesome dogs barking in the "icy hay" and coming up with a phrase like "icy hay" which is really good. I just came up with it now, trying to research back. You also get a better balance in the poem—better humor, better balance of attitude in what you're talking about. Just like *samatha*, wakefulness leads to *vipasyana*, detailed awareness, or awareness of detail around you, the space around you. So there seems to be that correlation of poetry, that practicing mindfulness in meditation provides haiku-like detail.

P.P.: *You've been writing a lot of haikus lately. In fact, many of the ones you've showed me come directly out of the meditation practices during and after retreats, like the King Sooper haiku in your new book* Mind Breaths.

A.G.: Something interesting here is that I went into a retreat in September, 1975, with the suggestion by Trungpa that I not do any writing while on the retreat. At first, when I heard the notion, it really offended me, thinking it was a philistine notion. But, on the other hand, when I came around to it, it seemed great because I realized I was obsessed with writing and transforming everything into writing and that obsession was inhibiting the writing. Not conducive to good writing. It was only conducive to a lot of mental friction, and self-consciousness, and inattentiveness to detail outside. So, I spent two weeks not writing. For the first time in thirty years, two weeks where, suddenly, I had the monkey of writing off my back! And it cleared a huge space in my head. Took a lot of anxiety away because I realized I was writing like a guilty Puritan or a guilty Protestant—you know, I felt that I had to write a poem all the time. That affected my seeing things because I was seeing things in terms of how you verbalize them.

P.P.: *Everything was immediately translated into words for poetry, or everything was poetry?*

A.G.: Well, no, not as good as that. It was looking at objects, always trying to verbalize them, like the trees waving in the late afternoon outside here: "trees waving in the later afternoon, breeze under the telegraph wires." Actually, it was just sort of stereotyping everything constantly into mind, into words. I was missing some finer, organic detail.

P.P.: *So what happened after two weeks of all-day meditation, without resorting to writing?*

A.G.: When I found that certain situations were so strong and pungent visually, I was able to remember them anyway—even if I didn't write it down; real perceptions, really acute imagist perceptions stayed with me without my having to work on it. The day I came out of the retreat, then I wrote down a whole series of situations, haiku situations. Very briefly, in ten minutes.

P.P.: *Things you felt or that occurred during meditation?*

A.G.: Haiku situations that occurred during the meditation which were so deep-rooted as insights that they stuck with me. I didn't have to worry about writing them down. I could always write them down later because they were permanent insight, like:

> Sitting on a tree stump with half a cup of tea,
> sun down behind the mountains—
> Nothing to do.

Or another one:

> Not a word! Not a word!
> Flies do all my talking for me—
> and the wind says something else.

Or

> Fly on my nose,
> I'm not the Buddha,
> There's no enlightenment here!

I was trying to get the fly to go away. [Laughs]

P.P.: *Those last two follow the tradition of Zen poetry: the famous fly always appears in haikus, often while the poet is sitting.*

A.G.: Yeah. So, this is my way of dealing with it. "I'm not the Buddha, go away!" [Laughs] "I'm not the glorious one, stay away from me!" Or here's one more:

> Against a red bark trunk
> A fly's shadow
> lights on the shadow of a pine bough.

That was a bit labored, but I actually saw the shadow of a fly.

P.P.: *But were you writing out of the Zen "fly" tradition . . .*

A.G.: I had read them, but, I mean, I had a *real* fly in front of my nose! And I was sitting for hours and started laughing when I realized—you know, by vanity, posing as a Buddha. I was just sort of making a joke, realization, of sitting, boring sitting and that I wasn't a Buddha! Here's one:

> An hour after dawn
> I haven't thought of Buddha yet!
> —walking back into the retreat house.

The day I got out, I wrote all those down. Then we drove to the King Supermarket, "King Sooper," and we walked in and the first thing I saw was:

> A thin redfaced pimpled boy
> stands alone minutes
> looking down into the ice cream bin.

It was like a Blakean "marks of weakness, marks of woe," you could see the relation between his pimples and his longing for the ice cream sweets.

P.P.: *I showed that haiku to some friends and they were astounded by the "suchness" of the Americana, twentieth century "marks of woe consciousness"* . . .

A.G.: Karma, karma exemplified.

P.P.: *In your book, the little pamphlet of work poems* Sad Dust Glories *there is that cutting through to the suchness, little epiphany-like poems like the "King Sooper" one* . . .

A.G.: Maybe, maybe some of them. In that book, I don't know how much I'll include in *Mind Breaths;* it's too fragmentary. I've written enough now that the new book will have just the best poems, not everything I've written. I will relegate lesser notations to a journal, a lot of the rhapsodic stuff that doesn't make sense, that doesn't hang together.

P.P.: *In all the different consciousness experimentation that you've done since 1948, starting out with your Blake visions, then the drug trips, the Indian trip, the mantra trip, how do you* . . .

A.G.: I don't see them quite as "trips." I don't even like the terminology of "trip." Or "experiment" either—it's too high-toned. It was all just sort of curiosity; one thing led to another, in a fairly sequential and logical way. Right from my own nature, though I think I got into a lot of different blind alleys, spending years dallying and suffering.

P.P.: *Like with drugs?*

A.G.: Not because of drugs, but because of attitudes of mind connected with drugs—like looking for a heaven. Or like taking my Blake visions so obsessively that it inhibited seeing any more visions. Or my taking the Blake ambition of wanting to be God so seriously, which is like heavy egotism, really. And taking the ambitiousness of that into acid trips—which gave me a lot of bad times. So I spent years suffering for nothing, in a way, wasting time. Useful, I suppose, because a lot of people did that and so, maybe, I made a trail through the woods. Avoid

151

that mountain of ego vision! [Laughs]

P.P.: *The focus of your new book seems to be the* dharma, *exemplifying and talking about* dharma. *Is that kind of . . .*

A.G.: I didn't *intend* that, but it seems to be the development—*dharma* preoccupation, the preoccupation I've had during the time of writing it. Trungpa's in it a lot, as a reference point.

P.P.: *There's also a different kind of confessional element in the book, like the poem "Ego Confession," which starts out with*

> I want to be known as the most brilliant man in America
> Introduced to Gyalwa Karmapa heir of the Whispered
>   Transmission Crazy Wisdom Practice Lineage
> as the secret young man who visited him and winked
>   anonymously decade ago in Gangtok
> Prepared the way for Dharma in America without
>   mentioning Dharma . . .

A.G.: I like that poem. I dig that, but it's tricky.

P.P.: *It's like a total, absolute honesty—without any accoutrements, without trying to impress, just nakedness.*

A.G.: Except it's sort of sly, I mean it's finally so I can get away with all that—because they're all poems, ultimately.

P.P.: *I remember a story that when you first wrote it you were afraid to show it to anyone, is that right?*

A.G.: Well, originally, I was writing it . . . Anne Waldman and I were in San Francisco at a concert of Cecil Taylor. I thought that what I was saying was so demeaning or—what do you call it—"politically unwise"—that I didn't want her to see it. It seemed like a revelation of a lot . . .

P.P.: *Naughty things . . . [Laughs]*

A.G.: Well, yeah, naughty hypocrisy . . .

P.P.: *Un-Buddhalike . . .*

A.G.: No, just hypocritical. I realized later that such embarrassments always prove to be signs that something is going on. Like a little space has been opened up. "Howl" was like that, in the sense that I didn't intend to show it to anyone, to my family. Maybe to Peter or something. Then a week later, it looks like an obviously emotional truth, so why not?

P.P.: *Trungpa, as you say, definitely does seem to loom throughout the book, like in the poem "What would you do if you lost it all?" That's the question Trungpa asked you when he saw you (in your apartment lobby in New York) carrying your harmonium case. What would you do if you lost it all?*

A.G.: I lost it already.

P.P.: *You've given up your "prophetic, messianic identity"? I think that's how you characterized your role as a poet once.*

A.G.: Yeah, that's lost, and I could give up my harmonium. I mean, it would be bad if the harmonium was just another prop, a crutch.

P.P.: *So, what we're talking about now is surrendering, in Trungpa's sense of it.*

A.G.: Yeah, that's the word. I haven't thought of it much in those terms. Somehow I don't like that word; it's too "ikky," the associations are too weird.

P.P.: *How about "giving up," letting go of ego, completely . . .*

A.G.: No, that's too self-virtuous. I think the process is more discoverable, like including more embarrassing reality as in the "Ego Confession" poem. I think "giving up" is including a more embarrassing reality. In other words, I'm including, in "Ego Confession," the thoughts and formulations that pass through my mind because it seemed too extravagant, like the idea in the first line of thinking I want to be known as the wisest or most brilliant man in America. Well, I did secretly have that image of myself . . .

P.P.: *"Did" or still do?*

A.G.: Probably "do." But to say so, in a serious context, would expose me to the absurdity of that ambition and the fact that it's simply not true. So, except by willing to say so, that does make me a little more brilliant! [Laughs] By willing to be so, playfully, without being scared of being stuck with it. It's just a

153

little aspect; it's a thought that becomes transparent. You don't have to be scared of it being there in your head. It turns out that everybody has that feeling, or sixteen million people have that feeling. So, it's a poem with sixteen million readers, instead of sixteen million people turning and saying "Ahhh, Ginsberg, ickkk!" In other words, it turns out to be a somewhat universal fantasy—wide enough, broad enough area, archetypal enough fantasies that other people see the humor of finally saying it. It takes the sting out of it now.

P.P.: *It's learning nonattachment to ego...*

A.G.: Well, learning nonattachment to specific facets of the image of myself that I created through my poetry and through my own mind, and to my friends. Learning to break those stereotypes, allowing those stereotypes to fall apart naturally.

P.P.: *There's one question I always wanted to ask you about your poetry. It's just that so much of it seems preoccupied with death and dying...*

A.G.: I guess it's because I'm so scared—or was so scared.

P.P.: *Has the Tibetan path, specifically something like the* Sattipathana *exercises on the dissolution of the body...*

A.G.: Well, one thing that is easier now is—since I don't feel that I have an immortal soul that can go to heaven, I'm no longer scared of a slip-up at the last minute and getting stuck in hell, which I was before, as in the "LSD" poem in 1959. ["Lysergic Acid" in *Kaddish and Other Poems*] That makes things a little easier. There isn't the obsessive image bearing down on me all the time—that on the deathbed I have to go break through and finally realize it isn't real. That will probably save a lot of suffering. I still am afraid of pain.

P.P.: *Are you still afraid of death?*

A.G.: I don't know, I'll worry about it when it happens. I seem to be able to relate to my father's dying with less hysteria than I would have before, with less impulse to lay a story on him. You know, let him die his own death without my imposing the *Tibetan Book of the Dead* on him, or something.

P.P.: *You've been teaching the idea of writing spontaneously to your students here at Naropa. Has the Tibetan influence entered into that notion as well?*

A.G.: I'm good at teaching it and formulating it, the idea of spontaneous composition.

P.P.: *You're good at doing it too, not having to write a crafted (in the Western sense of craft) poem, just letting it happen, naturally, spontaneously.*

A.G.: That was always a basic principle, to write a poem by not writing a poem. It is Williams' practice. So that was inculcated early in my poetry, especially in *Empty Mirror*. Things I didn't expect were important, turned out to be the best poetry because the spontaneous mind was more straightforward, full of strong detail.

P.P.: *The association I was trying to make is Trungpa's definition of poetic practice as "First Thought, Best Thought."*

A.G.: I'm not sure whether he said that first or me. I think he appropriated it, but we probably worked it out together. I am not sure. It does involve accepting your thoughts, being able to work with your own thoughts as they are, without preselecting the tendency that you want to emphasize, on account of a specific kind of spiritual bias. It's more like having an open mind about your own thoughts so that you don't formulate them into a romantic stream, just picking out the romantic ones or the apocalyptic ones or the anti-war ones or the self-humiliating ones or the self-glorifying ones. For instance,

> Not a word! Not a word!
> Flies do all my talking for me.

I think I would have been ashamed of that attitude twenty years ago. Not realizing how sharp it was. I would have admired it as a haiku, but I think I would have been ashamed of settling for that.

P.P.: *Why?*

A.G.: Because it means a failure in achieving cosmic vision. Except that it is obviously cosmic vision in a sense—it's actual. It means saying that anything I could say is no better than a fly's buzzing. The only stereotype there, is a certain renunciation of an ideal; renunciation of ideals are part of the surrender, so to speak. But looked at from a youthful point of view, that's really betrayal—like Wordsworth, or like Gregory's poem [Gregory Corso] "I Am 25":

> ... I HATE OLD POETMEN!
> Especially old poetmen who retract ...
> saying:—I did those then
> > but that was then
> > that was then—

The way he ends his poem

> Then at night in the confidence of their homes
> rip out their apology-tongues
> and steal their poems.

[Laughs] So he had a kind of double mind about that. He's regretted that poem, in a funny humorous way.

P.P.: *I remember at one point in your development you said that language itself might be a barrier to "suchness," to further awareness.*

A.G.: Well, that's a tradition. I was preoccupied with that notion in Burroughs' cut-ups in the 1960's.

P.P.: *Did the Tibetan practice help you out of that dilemma?*

A.G.: Trungpa said "Don't write a poem, don't take any writing with you. Don't bother your head with *language,* with formulating language. Don't bother your head with trying to solidify perceptions, prematurely ..."—really is what he was saying. I think it finally means let the perceptions flow as they come and write them down when you write—but don't be straining aggressively to solidify perceptions, just to have solidified perceptions on a piece of paper so you can have a poem and call yourself a poet! Which is just common sense, also.

P.P.: *Have you ever been hung up on trying to better your previous work. A lot of writers have one great masterpiece and then live in fear of it, always trying to outdo themselves.*

A.G.: I never did have very much of a preoccupation of having to equal early work—that's an obvious trap, a vulgar trap. And there are lots of examples, like Blake and people. Once they start an autobiographical curve, any point in it is interesting—because it's interesting. Even Whitman in his old age, just writing *Sands* at age seventy. He's writing the great *Leaves of Grass*, but he's also writing the necessary *Sands At Seventy!* Or old leaves from a tree. There was no need for Whitman to feel guilty that he's still not working on a new conception while he was falling apart. In fact, it was necessary to register his falling apart! Rather than maintaining a fixed-ness with things still building toward some orgasmic, youthful expostulation. I'm really interested in that in relation to Dylan and Lennon and the other pop artists who are always saddled with an image of having to surpass themselves, or equal themselves—constantly acused of *not* equalling themselves when they are manifesting themselves in their present form.

P.P.: *Everyone wants them to fail, claims they're copping out because they are not doing what they had been.*

A.G.: As if people want Dylan to die—you know, the apocalyptic death.

P.P.: *Like Rimbaud, or at least, like the "Myth of Rimbaud."*

A.G.: That's why I feel so sympathetic to Dylan, because it seems he's bearing this fantastic burden of image—in a very Zen way. Not at all entrapped in it. So heavy a weight that he couldn't possibly be attracted to it, or entrapped by it. And yet, not renouncing it. Neither grasping nor trying to deny—simply allowing his image its space, allowing himself his own space and not separating from it, but also not clinging to it. Because it's partly true, and he knows it's probably true. That's his good humor. So the constant play is just enjoying what's going on—in my head, or a broken bone, or not being able to get it up, or getting it up. In the best, if I stay in Whitman's old thing: "Do I contradict myself or do I contradict myself?"

P.P.: *"Very well, I contradict myself... I am multitudes!"*

A.G.: That's the way existence is. And that's an easy out, out from an over-rigid perplexity.

P.P.: *There's one last thing I want to get into. It seems that the parallels with the* vipasyana *technique and what seems to interest you in Williams and in a lot of other poetry is the ability to write down, exactly or as accurately as possible, what is happening right here and now. You said you admired William's dictum about concentrating on square, eye-on-the-thing reality—not ideas or abstractions, but on the things, existence itself, a poetry writing based on the here and now of quotidian reality . . .*

A.G.: Yeah, located or defined as here and now or quotidian reality because that's what people need, mostly. But when Williams is dancing in his attic, waving a shirt around his head, naked, admiring his body, saying "I'm lonely . . ."—that's also quotidian reality. It's not everybody's, but it's his. "Quotidian" in the sense that he's in his attic, and he's a family man, but everybody does that anyway. And it's also an extraordinary reality; so, quotidian reality really is extraordinary—a lot of it. It's actually discovering the goofiness of actuality, rather than the boring . . . or the goofiness of the boring actuality.

P.P.: *The suchness?*

A.G.: Well, yeah. The flavor of suchness is goofiness. That's what I mean by "goofiness." That's the way suchness appears—very often as "goofy." As Kerouacian, as Kerouacky.

P.P.: *Does sitting help you incorporate these Buddhist ideas into your poetry?*

A.G.: I don't correlate it too much, actually. I correlate *vipasyana* and *samatha* practice to poetry in the class I teach here at Naropa because it seems like a clear way of pointing out direction to a group of students involved in Buddhism, actually practicing these meditation techniques, as I am. But I don't necessarily think of the correlations—it's too logical to put it down like that.

P.P.: *Too one-to-one? Too simplistic?*

A.G.: Yeah, too one-to-one. Really, the best advice is mellow character—rather than *vipasyana*. [Laughs] It means the same thing, accommodating humor, mellow character toward one's quirks—and others'. Like my ideal in poetry, or "Buddhist poetry," was: "the autumn moon shines kindly on the flower thief."

P.P.: *Issa?*

A.G.: Yeah, I'm misquoting it, but it goes something like that. It is like Whitman's "Not until the sun rejects you, do I reject you." Awareness continually shining or mellow accommodation-mind continually shining. It's somewhat equivalent to Buddhist terminology, but I think it's more Americanese when you say "mellow"—more understandable. "Mellow character," the ideal of which is W. C. Fields—in a way. [Laughs] Yeah, the Fieldsian aspects of accommodation . . .

P.P.: *Playfulness . . .*

A.G.: Yeah, noticing detail, and—at the same time—surprised, horrified, and shocked; you are humoring one's extremist reactions. One of the things I do in class is try and make all these Buddhist correlations, trying to make it orderly and rational, but not making it too packaged, too Buddhist-like. At the same time, some of the Buddhist parallels fit, like Williams' poem "Thursday," or the descriptions of *samatha* leading to *vipasyana,* or attention and wakefulness leading to minute observation of detail. The parallels are useful reference points, but, maybe, impracticable in a sense.

P.P.: *Has meditation helped you achieve a finer, more detailed perception of reality, opened you up to clear perception—in the Buddhist sense of not laying your interpretation on the actual reality?*

A.G.: I don't think so, hell, I don't know. [Laughs] I really can't tell or measure it because I already had the idea of experiencing detail and chasing it around since the early 1950's. At this point, it has made me more relaxed about *chasing* details. [Laughs] I was always too heavy-handed and too theoretical about this—you can't really chase details—you have to remember them, experience them and then remember them, rather than chase after the perfect detail. You have to learn to see things, but without always the self-consciousness of noticing this detail and that one. It's more like a real process of recollection rather than automatic attention—so it's attention to your recollections, maybe. Attention to recollection, in the sense of seeing something curious, like "the icy hay"—funny sound, interesting image, clear . . . goofy! "Icy hay in the barn, the dogs lying in the icy hay in the barn . . ." In trying to describe that situation, I wound up with "icy hay"; then, a second later, I realized "icy hay"—ah, that's interesting, that's really interesting, I really got it. But I didn't realize I got it when I got it! It was only after a moment of recollection. Most haikus and most poetry, most images are recollections of an instant, the thought of an instant ago or a minute ago or maybe an hour ago or a year ago—the picture comes up that you hadn't paid attention to.

P.P.: *Does that conflict with the notion of spontaneity, recollection versus spontaneity.*

A.G.: Well, recollecting is something you can't do on purpose, it just comes up spontaneously. Recollection is spontaneous by itself. "Spontaneous" means allowing the mind to . . . remembering the mind, remembering the mind's activities. And, using that, the mind's recollections, as a subject, using that kind of attention as a subject—rather than a more fixated thing like having to write down everything that's happening right on the street, right this minute. Or the attitude: "I gotta write it down for a sonnet. I gotta have an idea about life and write it down in the form of a sonnet." So, the poetry is natural that way and becomes a natural product of awareness, rather than a crafty synthesis—crafty synthesis because you're synthesizing your recollections. Maybe I'm just kicking a dead horse.

P.P.: *The use of spontaneity in writing songs, as Milarepa practiced and as you do now in your collection of songs, would be the ultimate in that practice . . .*

A.G.: There's a very nice song in *Loka II* that I wrote spontaneously, spontaneously recollecting the events of a recent illness. It comes at the point in a conversation between

William Burroughs, Trungpa, myself, and other people when Trungpa asks me to make up a song, on the spot. I did and it was typed up later. It's not bad, actually.

P.P.: *How does it begin?*

A.G.:

> Started doing my prostrations sometime in February '75
> Began flying as if I were alive
> In a long transmission consciousness felt quite good and true
> But then I got into a sweat while thinkin' about you,
> Fell down with bronchitis, the first illness that came
> Pneumonia in the hospital was what they said was the name . . .

It's actually pretty humorous for such a serious set of events. Writing spontaneously while recollecting—I had to accept *any* thought. The whole point of spontaneous improvisation in song is that you have to accept whatever thought presents itself to your rhyme—on the wing, so to speak. Otherwise, you have to break the rhythm, stop the song, start thinking. Once you do that, you're lost. You have to keep the impulse going—accept doggerel as well as beauty because you are improvising and relying on the moment to moment inspiration. It means relying on moment to moment ordinary mind, whatever rises. It's absolutely necessary to take whatever you can get, if you're singing; settle for what's there, at the instant—otherwise, you break the chain. I do think *samatha* practice does help there because you become more minutely aware of what's rising in the mind, thought forms rising and disappearing. And you learn to look on them with less prejudice than before—like this thought is good and that thought's bad. Any thought will do! When you get to that equality of temperament or judgment, all the thoughts turn out to have their place, to form a sort of recognizable pattern or chain of workable thoughts—as Trungpa says, "workable."

P.P.: *That must take a tremendous ability of self-acceptance.*

A.G.: I think it's much easier than you think. It's fun! [Laughs] Fun in the sense of being with good friends, drinking and making up songs. You let your tongue go loose! Everybody accommodates to that. Nobody's embarrassed by anything.

161

There's less anxiety once you've realized that there's nothing you can do about it. Why fight it? You can't change your mind—your mind is its own. And there's nothing heroic about that acceptance. Nor do I think it's a transition to another state of consciousness. That's the whole point—it's ordinary mind! The question is "Do you accept ordinary mind or not?" But even that question is too much of an either/or proposition. It's more like "Do you recognize what ordinary mind is?" That's where the problem is, not willing to recognize it, to having to be turned on to it. Most people don't recognize their ordinary mind; they use it all the time, but they use it selectively, just for certain highlights to fix up a specific thought pattern, image, ambition. They think that ordinary mind is just certain highlights or ordinary mind, rather than the whole thing.

P.P.: *But in Western art and poetry, the tradition demands that one respect the idea of high thoughts, like "What was so often thought, but never so well expressed."*

A.G.: Well, it's true! I agree with that—just express what is so often thought.

P.P.: *But what to do with doggerel, the superficial—it wouldn't be very good poetry with all the ordinary mind trivial flow.*

A.G.: That's too academic and stylized and way off in the distance. Nobody really takes that attitude too seriously.

P.P.: *I'm not so sure.*

A.G.: You shouldn't isolate what you do every day, all day. Anyway, there isn't much difference, it's just a question of learning a sharper, more experienced way of recognizing and appreciating what's already in your head. It doesn't require a big breakthrough or anything like that.

P.P.: *Stop trying to have visions . . .*

A.G.: One wants to have visions because one thinks that one's ordinary reality, ordinary consciousness is not visionary enough. Which is a big stink everybody has about themselves—everybody—that their body is awful, their mind is awful. Being who you are is awful enough without being *that* awful!

FOOTNOTES

Preface

1. Ginsberg, journal poem shown to me in July, 1976.
2. Allen Ginsberg, from a letter to John Hollander, 1958.
3. William Blake, *The Poetry and Prose of William Blake*, ed. David Erdman (New York: Doubleday and Company, 1965), p. 680.
4. Plotinus, *The Enneads* (London: Faber and Faber, 1962), p. 409.
5. Oswald Spengler, *The Decline of the West* (New York: Alfred Knopf, 1961), p. 95.
6. William Blake, *The Poetry and Prose of William Blake*, p. 38.
7. Alexander Gilchrist, *Life of William Blake* (New Jersey: Rowan and Littlefield, 1973), p. 7.
8. Allen Ginsberg, "The Art of Poetry VIII," *The Paris Review*, 10, 37 (Spring 1966), p. 36.

Introduction

1. Allen Ginsberg, "When The Mode of the Music Changes the Walls of the City Shake," *The Second Coming Magazine*, I, 2 (July, 1961), p. 40.

2. Allen Ginsberg, "Craft Interview With Allen Ginsberg," in *The Craft of Poetry,* ed. William Packard (New York: Doubleday and Company, 1974), p. 69.

3. Allen Ginsberg, *Mystery in the Universe: notes on an interview with Allen Ginsberg,* ed. Edward Lucie-Smith (London: Turret Books, 1965), p. 6.

Chapter 1

1. Allen Ginsberg, from a manuscript shown to me by Ginsberg in July, 1976.

2. Allen Ginsberg, "Psalm IV," *The Floating Bear: a newsletter,* No. 32 (1966), p. 7.

3. Allen Ginsberg, *The Visions of the Great Rememberer* (Massachusetts: Mulch Press, 1974), p. 55.

4. Ginsberg, "The Art of Poetry VIII," p. 36.

5. Ginsberg, p. 35.

6. Allen Ginsberg, *The Gates of Wrath, Rhymed Poems: 1948– 1952* (Bolinas: Grey Fox Press, 1972), p. 11.

7. Ginsberg, from an early journal.

8. Ginsberg, "The Art of Poetry VIII," p. 37.

9. Ginsberg, p. 36.

10. Ginsberg, p. 36.

11. Ginsberg, p. 36.

12. Ginsberg, p. 36.

13. Ginsberg, p. 37.

14. Ginsberg, p. 37.

15. Ginsberg, p. 37.

16. Ginsberg, p. 37.

17. Allen Ginsberg, from an unpublished interview conducted by Paul Portugés, July, 1976.

18. Ginsberg, "The Art of Poetry VIII," p. 37.

19. Ginsberg, p. 38.

20. Ginsberg, p. 38.

21. Ginsberg, p. 38.

22. Ginsberg, Unpublished Interview with Paul Portugés.

23. Ginsberg, "The Art of Poetry VIII," p. 38.

24. Ginsberg, p. 38.

25. Ginsberg, from a notebook entry describing Blake's poems.

26. Ginsberg, "The Art of Poetry VIII," p. 39.

27. Ginsberg, p. 39.

28. Ginsberg, p. 40.

29. Ginsberg, p. 39.

30. Ginsberg, p. 40.

31. Ginsberg, p. 40.

32. Ginsberg, p. 40.

33. Ginsberg, p. 42.

34. Ginsberg, p. 42.

35. Ginsberg, p. 43.

36. Ginsberg, p. 43.

37. Ginsberg, p. 44.

38. Ginsberg, p. 45.

39. Ginsberg, p. 45.

40. Ginsberg, *Gates of Wrath,* quoted as an epigraph, no pagination.

41. Allen Ginsberg, *Allen Verbatim,* ed. Gordon Ball (New York: McGraw-Hill, 1974), p. 21.

42. Ginsberg, p. 21.

Chapter II

1. Allen Ginsberg, unpublished poem shown to me in July 1976.

2. Ginsberg, *Gates of Wrath,* p. 16.

3. Allen Ginsberg, *Kaddish and Other Poems: 1958–1960* (San Francisco: City Lights Books, 1961), p. 53.

4. Allen Ginsberg, Unpublished Interview, July 1976.

5. Blake, *The Poetry and Prose of William Blake,* p. 696.

6. Blake, p. 144.

7. Allen Ginsberg, "Notes Written on Finally Recording 'Howl'," in *A Casebook On The Beat,* ed. Thomas Parkinson (New York: Thomas Y. Crowell Company, 1961), p. 28.

8. Ginsberg, *Gates of Wrath,* p. 4.

9. Ginsberg, Unpublished Interview, July 1976.

10. Ginsberg, *Gates of Wrath,* p. 3.

11. Ginsberg, *Allen Verbatim,* p. 139.

12. S. Foster Damon, *A Blake Dictionary: The Ideas and Symbols of William Blake* (New York: E. P. Dutton & Co., 1971), p. 331.

13. Ginsberg, Unpublished Interview, July 1976.
14. Ginsberg, *Gates of Wrath*, p. 7.
15. Ginsberg, Unpublished Interview, July 1976.
16. Ginsberg, letter to Van Doren.
17. Ginsberg, *Gates of Wrath*, p. 7.
18. Ginsberg, Unpublished Interview, July 1976.
19. Ginsberg, Unpublished Interview, July 1976.
20. Ginsberg, *Gates of Wrath*, p. 18.
21. Ginsberg, p. 19.
22. Ginsberg, Unpublished Interview, July 1976.
23. Ginsberg, Unpublished Interview, July 1976.
24. Ginsberg, Unpublished Interview, July 1976.
25. Ginsberg, *Gates of Wrath*, p. 41.
26. Ginsberg, p. 41.
27. Ginsberg, p. 55.
28. Ginsberg, Unpublished Interview, July 1976.
29. Ginsberg, Unpublished Interview, July 1976.
30. Ginsberg, "The Art of Poetry VIII," p. 38.
31. Ginsberg, *Allen Verbatim*, p. 140.
32. Allen Ginsberg, *Empty Mirror* (New York: Totem Press in association with Corinth Books, 1961), p. 14.
33. Ginsberg, *Allen Verbatim*, p. 141.
34. Ginsberg, *Empty Mirror*, p. 31.
35. Ginsberg, *Allen Verbatim*, p. 140.
36. Ginsberg, *Empty Mirror*, p. 19.
37. Ginsberg, Unpublished Interview, July 1976.
38. Ginsberg, *Allen Verbatim*, p. 142.
39. Ginsberg, p. 142.
40. Ginsberg, Unpublished Interview, July 1976.
41. Ginsberg, p. 106.
42. Ginsberg, Unpublished Interview, July 1976.
43. Ginsberg, Unpublished Interview, July 1976.
44. Ginsberg, *Allen Verbatim*, p. 143.
45. Ginsberg, *Empty Mirror*, p. 19.
46. Allen Ginsberg, *Reality Sandwiches* (San Francisco: City Lights Books, 1963), p. 40.
47. Allen Ginsberg, *The Fall of America: Poems Of These States* (San Francisco: City Lights Books, 1972), p. 55.
48. Ginsberg, Unpublished Interview, July 1976.
49. Blake, *The Poetry and Prose of William Blake*, p. 39.

Chapter III

1. Unpublished poem from a manuscript shown to me by Ginsberg, June 1976.
2. Ginsberg, Unpublished Interview, July 1976.
3. Ginsberg, "The Art of Poetry VIII," p. 39.
4. Ginsberg, from a notebook entry describing Blake's poems.
5. Ginsberg, *Gates of Wrath*, p. 3.
6. Ginsberg, p. 3.
7. Ginsberg, p. 3.
8. Ginsberg, *Empty Mirror*, p. 13.
9. Ginsberg, p. 24.
10. Ginsberg, p. 40.
11. Ginsberg, *Reality Sandwiches*, p. 7.
12. Ginsberg, p. 33.
13. Ginsberg, p. 41.
14. Allen Ginsberg, *Howl and Other Poems* (San Francisco: City Lights Books, 1956), pp. 11–12.
15. Ginsberg, p. 31.
16. Ginsberg, *Kaddish*, p. 40.
17. Ginsberg, from a journal.
18. Ginsberg, from a journal. The blank space indicated by parentheses has been copied exactly as it appears in a green notebook dated 1948.
19. Unpublished poem from a manuscript shown to me by Ginsberg.
20. Ginsberg, *Kaddish*, p. 83.
21. Ginsberg, p. 100.
22. Ginsberg, *Empty Mirror*, p. 40.
23. Ginsberg, p. 40.
24. Ginsberg, p. 40.
25. Ginsberg, p. 40.
26. Ginsberg, p. 40.
27. Ginsberg, p. 40.
28. Ginsberg, *Howl*, p. 21.
29. Ginsberg, *Kaddish*, p. 36.
30. Ginsberg, p. 32.
31. Ginsberg, *Howl*, p. 28.
32. Ginsberg, p. 30.
33. Ginsberg, p. 30.

34. Allen Ginsberg, *Prose Contribution to Cuban Revolution* (Detroit: Workshop Press, 1966), no pagination.

35. Allen Ginsberg, "First Thought, Best Thought," *Loka I*, 1 (1975), p. 89.

36. Allen Ginsberg, "A Conversation With Allen Ginsberg," ed. Paul Geneson, *Chicago Review*, 27, 1 (Summer, 1975), p. 27.

37. Ginsberg, p. 27.

38. Ginsberg, *Empty Mirror*, p. 45.

39. Ginsberg, Unpublished Interview, July 1976.

40. Ginsberg, Unpublished Interview, July 1976.

41. Ginsberg, *Allen Verbatim*, p. 145–146.

42. Jack Kerouac, "Essentials of Spontaneous Prose," *Evergreen Review*, Vol. 2, No. 5 (Summer, 1958), p. 72.

43. Jack Kerouac, "Belief & Technique for Modern Prose," *Evergreen Review*, Vol. 2, No. 8 (Spring, 1959), p. 57.

44. Kerouac, p. 57.

45. Ginsberg, "Craft Interview With Allen Ginsberg," p. 57.

46. Ginsberg, p. 59.

47. Ginsberg, "When The Mode of the Music Changes the Walls of the City Shake," p. 40.

48. Kerouac, "Belief & Technique for Modern Prose," p. 57.

49. Ginsberg, "Craft Interview With Allen Ginsberg," p. 61.

50. Ginsberg, *Allen Verbatim*, p. 144.

51. Ginsberg, p. 147.

52. Ginsberg, "Craft Interview With Allen Ginsberg," p. 73.

Chapter IV

1. Ginsberg, from a journal notation.

2. Ginsberg, *Kaddish*, p. 93.

3. Ginsberg, "Craft Interview With Allen Ginsberg," p. 65.

4. Ginsberg, "The Art of Poetry VIII," p. 39.

5. Ginsberg, p. 40.

6. Ginsberg, p. 44.

7. Ginsberg, "Craft Interview With Allen Ginsberg," p. 72.

8. Ginsberg, from a journal.

9. Ginsberg, from one of Ginsberg's notebooks. It is taken from Blake's notes on Watson: "Every honest man is a prophet..."

10. Damon, *A Blake Dictionary*, p. 335.

11. Damon, p. 335.
12. Ginsberg, Ginsberg Collection.
13. Ginsberg, *Allen Verbatim*, p. 104.
14. Ginsberg, "Craft Interview With Allen Ginsberg," p. 65.
15. Ginsberg, p. 65.
16. Ginsberg, p. 70.
17. Ginsberg, *Gates of Wrath*, p. 16.
18. Ginsberg, *Empty Mirror*, p. 9.
19. Ginsberg, p. 25.
20. Ginsberg, p. 25.
21. Ginsberg, p. 9.
22. Ginsberg, p. 11.
23. Ginsberg, p. 11.
24. Ginsberg, *Reality Sandwiches*, p. 24.
25. Ginsberg, p. 33.
26. Ginsberg, p. 62.
27. Ginsberg, from a journal notation.
28. Allen Ginsberg, "A Talk With Allen Ginsberg," ed. Alison Colbert, *Partisan Review*, XXXVI, No. 3 (1971), p. 301.
29. Ginsberg, *Reality Sandwiches*, p. 62.
30. Ginsberg, *Kaddish*, pp. 90–91.
31. Ginsberg, p. 93.
32. Ginsberg, "The Art of Poetry VIII," p. 39.
33. Ginsberg, *Kaddish*, p. 93.
34. Ginsberg, p. 93.
35. Ginsberg, "Craft Interview With Allen Ginsberg," p. 66.
36. Ginsberg, p. 73.
37. Ginsberg, p. 72.
38. Ginsberg, p. 73.
39. Ginsberg, p. 73.
40. Ginsberg, p. 73.
41. Ginsberg, p. 73.
42. Ginsberg, p. 73.
43. Ginsberg, *Reality Sandwiches*, p. 42.
44. Ginsberg, p. 42.
45. Ginsberg, p. 44.
46. Ginsberg, p. 44.
47. Ginsberg, *Gates of Wrath*, pp. 34–35.
48. Ginsberg, *Reality Sandwiches*, p. 39.
49. Ginsberg, *Howl*, p. 25.
50. Ginsberg, p. 37.

51. Ginsberg, from a manuscript shown to me by Ginsberg, June 1976.

52. Ginsberg, *Improvised Poetics,* ed. Mark Robison (San Francisco: Anonym Press, 1971), p. 22.

53. Ginsberg, "A Talk With Allen Ginsberg," p. 297.

54. Ginsberg, "Notes on Finally Recording 'Howl'," p. 29.

55. Ginsberg, *Improvised Poetics,* p. 22.

56. Ginsberg, "A Talk With Allen Ginsberg," p. 297.

57. Ginsberg, *Howl,* p. 17.

58. Ginsberg, *Allen Verbatim,* p. 23.

59. Ginsberg, p. 28.

60. Ginsberg, p. 109.

61. Ginsberg, p. 47.

62. Allen Ginsberg, "How *Kaddish* Happened," in *The Poetics of the New American Poetry,* ed. Donald Allen and Warren Tallman (New York: Grove Press, Inc., 1973), p. 347.

63. Ginsberg, *Kaddish,* p. 27.

64. Ginsberg, Unpublished Interview, July 1976.

65. This use of breath and its parallel to thought was something Olson demanded in his essay "Projective Verse."

66. Allen Ginsberg, *Planet News* (San Francisco: City Lights Books, 1968), pp. 123–124.

67. Ginsberg, *Improvised Poetics,* p. 14.

68. Ginsberg, p. 4.

69. Ginsberg, "Craft Interview with Allen Ginsberg," p. 73.

70. Ginsberg, p. 73.

71. Ginsberg, p. 73.

72. Ginsberg, p. 73.

73. Ginsberg, p. 73.

74. Ginsberg, p. 73.

75. Jeremiah, *The Lamentations of Jeremiah,* in *Holy Bible* (Chicago: National Publishing Co., 1961), p. 732.

76. Christopher Smart, "Jubilate Agno," in *The Norton Anthology of Poetry* (Revised Shorter Edition), ed. Alexander Allison, *et al.* (New York: W. W. Norton & Company, 1975), p. 212.

77. Ginsberg, "Craft Interview With Allen Ginsberg," p. 77.

78. Ginsberg, *Empty Mirror,* p. 39.

79. Ginsberg, *Improvised Poetics,* p. 31.

80. Ginsberg, from Ginsberg manuscript, Ginsberg Collection, Columbia University.

81. Ginsberg, "Notes on Finally Recording 'Howl'," p. 28.

82. Ginsberg, p. 28.
83. Ginsberg, *Improvised Poetics*, p. 31.

Chapter V

1. Ginsberg, "The Art of Poetry VIII," p. 50.
2. Ginsberg, *Allen Verbatim*, p. 20.
3. Ginsberg, Unpublished Interview, July 1976.
4. Ginsberg, "The Art of Poetry VIII," p. 45.
5. Ginsberg, p. 45.
6. Ginsberg, "The Art of Poetry VIII," p. 48.
7. Ginsberg, p. 48.
8. Ginsberg, p. 48.
9. Ginsberg, p. 48.
10. Ginsberg, p. 48.
11. Ginsberg, p. 49.
12. Ginsberg, p. 49.
13. Ginsberg, Unpublished Interview, July 1976.
14. Ginsberg, Unpublished Interview, July 1976.
15. Ginsberg, *Indian Journals* (San Francisco: Dave Haselwood Books and City Lights Books, 1970), p. 4.
16. Ginsberg, "The Art of Poetry VIII," pp. 49–50.
17. Ginsberg, p. 50.
18. Ginsberg, p. 50.
19. Ginsberg, p. 50.
20. Ginsberg, *Planet News*, p. 62.
21. David Cooper, *The Grammar of Living* (New York: Pantheon Books, 1974), p. 143.
22. Ginsberg, *Planet News*, p. 62.
23. Ginsberg, p. 62.
24. Ginsberg, p. 59.
25. Ginsberg, p. 61.
26. Ginsberg, p. 62.
27. Ginsberg, "The Art of Poetry VIII," p. 50.
28. Ginsberg, p. 50.
29. Ginsberg, p. 50.
30. "Groundedness" is a term frequently used by Ginsberg's Tibetan guru, Chögyam Trungpa. Essentially, it means accepting things as they are, to stop conjuring romantic, unreal, or metaphysical realities and just "ground" oneself in the quotidian world of living and dying.

31. Ginsberg, from an unpublished interview in 1964 conducted by Bruce Kawain on the Columbia University Radio Station.

Chapter VI

1. Ginsberg, Unpublished Interview, July 1976.
2. Ginsberg, from a manuscript shown to me by Ginsberg, June 1976.
3. Ginsberg, Unpublished Interview, July 1976.
4. Ginsberg, "The Art of Poetry VIII," p. 41.
5. Ginsberg, *Howl*, p. 11.
6. Blake, *The Poetry and Prose of William Blake*, p. 37.
7. Blake, p. 38.
8. Ginsberg, "The Art of Poetry VIII," p. 37.
9. Ginsberg, p. 37.
10. Ginsberg told me it was practically impossible to make such one-to-one parallels (in a conversation on June 12, 1976).
11. Plotinus, *The Enneads*, p. 409.
12. Mircea Eliade, *The Two and The One* (New York: Harper & Row, 1965), p. 21.
13. St. John of the Cross, *The Mystical Doctrine of St. John of the Cross* (London: Sheed & Ward, 1948), p. 6.
14. Ginsberg, *Allen Verbatim*, p. 16.
15. Ginsberg, p. 16.
16. St. John of the Cross, *The Mystical Doctrine*, p. 23.
17. Ginsberg, "The Art of Poetry VIII," p. 35.
18. Ginsberg, *Allen Verbatim*, p. 16.
19. Evelyn Underhill, *Mysticism* (New York: E. P. Dutton & Co., 1961), pp. 266–297.
20. St. John of the Cross, *The Mystical Doctrine*, p. 38.
21. Underhill, *Mysticism*, p. 270.

SELECTED BIBLIOGRAPHY

The following list is by no means exhaustive. It contains only the most important collections of Ginsberg's poetry and prose (in addition to a few secondary sources referred to in the text) that are directly related to this study. The reader should be aware of the massive collection of Ginsberg's papers on deposit at the Columbia University Library. It includes notebooks, workbooks, letters, books, newspaper clippings, diaries, photographs, records, *et al.*

Damon, S. Foster. *A Blake Dictionary: The Ideas and Symbols of William Blake.* New York: E. P. Dutton & Co., 1971.

Cooper, David. *The Grammar of Living.* New York: Pantheon Books, 1974.

Dowden, George. *A Bibliography of Works by Allen Ginsberg: October, 1943 to July 1, 1967.* San Francisco: City Lights Books, 1971.

Eliade, Mircea. *The Two and The One.* New York: Harper & Row, 1965.

Ginsberg, Allen. "A Conversation With Allen Ginsberg." Ed. Paul Geneson. *Chicago Review,* 27, 1 (Summer, 1975), pp. 27–35.

————. *Allen Verbatim: Lectures on Poetry, Politics, Consciousness.* Ed. Gordon Ball. New York: McGraw Hill, 1964.

————. "A Talk With Allen Ginsberg." Ed. Alison Colbert. *Partisan Review*, XXXVI, No. 3 (1971), pp. 289–302.

————. "Craft Interview With Allen Ginsberg." *The Craft of Poetry*. Ed. William Packard. New York: Doubleday, 1974, pp. 53–78.

————. *Empty Mirror: Early Poems*. New York: Totem Press in association with Corinth Books, 1961.

————. "First Thought, Best Thought." *Loka I*, 1 (1975), pp. 89–95.

————. "How *Kaddish* Happened." *The Poetics of the New American Poetry*. Ed. Donald Allen and Warren Tallman. New York: Grove Press, Inc., 1973, pp. 344–347.

————. *Howl and Other Poems*. San Francisco: City Lights Books, 1956.

————. *Indian Journals: March 1962–May 1963*. San Francisco: Dave Haselwood and City Lights Books, 1970.

————. *Kaddish and Other Poems: 1958–1960*. San Francisco: City Lights Books, 1961.

————. *Mystery in the Universe: notes on an interview with Allen Ginsberg*. Ed. Edward Lucie-Smith. London: Turret Books, 1965.

————. "Notes Written on Finally Recording 'Howl'." *A Casebook on the Beat*. Ed. Thomas Parkinson. New York: Thomas Y. Crowell Company, 1961, pp. 27–30.

————. *Planet News: 1961–1967*. San Francisco: City Lights Books, 1968.

————. *Prose Contribution to Cuban Revolution*. Detroit: Workshop Press, 1966.

————. "Psalm IV." *The Floating Bear: a newsletter*, No. 32 (1966), p. 7.

————. *Reality Sandwiches: 1953–1960*. San Francisco: City Lights Books, 1963.

————. "The Art of Poetry VIII." *The Paris Review*, 10, 37 (Spring 1966), pp. 13–55.

————. *The Fall of America: poems of these states, 1965–1971*. San Francisco: City Lights Books, 1972.

————. *The Gates of Wrath: Rhymed Poems, 1948–1952*. Bolinas: Grey Fox Press, 1972.

————. "When the Mode of the Music Changes the Walls of the City Shake." *The Second Coming Magazine*, I, 2 (July, 1961), pp. 40–42.

Jeremiah. *The Lamentations of Jeremiah. Holy Bible*. Chicago: National Publishing Co., 1961, pp. 729–734.

Kerouac, Jack. "Belief and Technique for Modern Prose." *Evergreen Review*, Vol. 2, No. 8 (Spring, 1959), p. 57.

—————. "Essentials of Spontaneous Prose." *Evergreen Review*, Vol. 2, No. 5 (Summer, 1958), pp. 72–73.

Milton, John. *Paradise Lost. The Norton Anthology of English Literature*. Vol. I. Ed. M. H. Abrams, *et al.* New York: W. W. Norton, 1962, pp. 914 ff.

Princeton Encyclopedia of Poetry and Poetics. Ed. Alex Preminger, *et al.* Princeton: Princeton University Press, 1965, p. 619.

Smart, Christopher. "Jubilate Agno." *The Norton Anthology of Poetry*. Revised Shorter Edition. Ed. Alexander Allison, *et al.* New York: W. W. Norton & Co., 1975, pp. 212–214.

St. John of the Cross. *The Mystical Doctrine of St. John of the Cross*. London: Sheed and Ward, 1948.

Underhill, Evelyn. *Mysticism*. New York: E. P. Dutton & Co., 1961.

Index

179

181